CL 6/10

2 8 AUG 2013   1 7 OCT 20

CW00537237

Chivalry-Now

The Code of Male Ethics

LD 4179753 1

First published by O Books, 2010
O Books is an imprint of John Hunt Publishing Ltd., The Bothy, Deershot Lodge, Park Lane, Ropley,
Hants, SO24 0BE, UK
office1@o-books.net
www.o-books.net

Distribution in:	South Africa
	Stephan Phillips (pty) Ltd
UK and Europe	Email: orders@stephanphillips.com
Orca Book Services	Tel: 27 21 4489839 Telefax: 27 21 4479879
orders@orcabookservices.co.uk	
Tel: 01202 665432 Fax: 01202 666219	Text copyright D. Joseph Jacques 2009
Int. code (44)	
	Design: Susan Poole
USA and Canada	
NBN	ISBN: 978 1 84694 284 6
custserv@nbnbooks.com	
Tel: 1 800 462 6420 Fax: 1 800 338 4550	All rights reserved. Except for brief quotations
	in critical articles or reviews, no part of this
Australia and New Zealand	book may be reproduced in any manner without
Brumby Books	prior written permission from the publishers.
sales@brumbybooks.com.au	
Tel: 61 3 9761 5535 Fax: 61 3 9761 7095	The rights of D. Joseph Jacques as author have
	been asserted in accordance with the
Far East (offices in Singapore, Thailand,	Copyright, Designs and Patents Act 1988.
Hong Kong, Taiwan)	
Pansing Distribution Pte Ltd	
kemal@pansing.com	A CIP catalogue record for this book is available
Tel: 65 6319 9939 Fax: 65 6462 5761	from the British Library.

Printed by Digital Book Print

O Books operates a distinctive and ethical publishing philosophy in
all areas of its business, from its global network of authors to
production and worldwide distribution.

Chivalry-Now

The Code of Male Ethics

D. Joseph Jacques

BOOKS

Winchester, UK
Washington, USA

LEEDS LIBRARIES AND INFORMATION SERVICE	
LD 4179753 1	
HJ	21-Jun-2010
646.7	£11.99
S035179/20A	

CONTENTS

Introduction: No Man's Land   1

1   Chivalry   10
2   Upon My Honor...   14
3   The Inner Source of Chivalry   19
4   I Will Develop My Life...   23
5   Character Above Riches...   31
6   Never Boast, but Cherish Humility...   39
7   Speak the Truth...   50
8   Defend those in need...   65
9   Honor and Respect Women...   79
10 I Will Uphold Justice...   98
11 Faithful in Love...   108
12 Abhor Scandals and Gossip...   125
13 Generous to the Poor...   137
14 I Will Forgive...   151
15 Courtesy and Honor...   158
16 The Quest   165
17 The Knight and His Sword   171
18 Dualism   184
19 The Future of Chivalry-Now   189

Epilogue   193

Dedication:

To my loving wife, Lynne, who believed in me
even when I did not.
To Arthur, whose shadow accompanied me
throughout this quest.
To my proof-readers who made the final rendition possible.
To my Companions from around the world, for whom
Chivalry-Now is more than just an idea, but a way of life.

INTRODUCTION

Trapped in No Man's Land

What does it mean to be a man?

This is surely one of the most significant questions we face — and one of the least considered, reflecting a functional void in our mainstream culture.

Coming from a lengthy career in social services, I firmly believe that almost all our social, political and family problems flow directly from our inability to fill that void. Its influence effects us all, shaping how we relate to one another and how we treat the world around us.

This is not just a male issue. Its ramifications affect both genders, because all our lives are interconnected. In the words of Martin Luther King, "I can never be what I ought to be until you are what you ought to be."

This relates not only to matters of race but to gender as well. While positive examples of manhood can still be found here and there, they are deterred by a pervasive mindset that neither propagates nor recognizes it.

In America, we shy away from defining manhood as if the very subject were taboo. After a long history of unwarranted violence and discrimination, men are being taught from birth that they automatically carry an inheritance of guilt for past sins. We make sure that no male child slips by without taking his share. Each of us is expected to bear the guilt of our forefathers along with a personal stigma for simply being male. We are told in a thousand different ways, either in silence or in the commercial media, that there is something inherently wrong with being a man.

The intent is clear. We do not want today's men repeating the crimes of the past. The hope seems to be that by tearing us from any sense of cultural identity the world can move toward greater harmony. More guilt and less pride make for a calmer species. Women and minorities will be treated better. The demise of Western male dominance might even bring an end to war.

Such conclusions are dangerously simplistic. We cannot excise the cultural identity of half the population like a cancer and replace it with nothing. Doing so sends our entire cultural evolution into a tailspin, leaving a psychic void that can only lead to disaster.

The results are all around us — a population of boys and men searching for who they are and how they fit in. No road map, no gender specific guidelines, no rite-of-passage — not even an articulated goal. Finding no guidance at all, many turn to whatever distraction is available, be it entertainment, business, sports or narcotics. Or they just give up.

Through diversionary substitutes they are introduced to poorly contrived role models:

Movie heroes, mostly dysfunctional, yet always scripted to come out on top. Selfish, angry, violent, often brutal, they appeal to those whose real cultural identity is sadly unformed. At the same time, the entertainment industry pushes socially accepted limits with sexual innuendo, foul language, and in-your-face aggression. They often appeal to the angry animus of young men, who do not understand the fundamental source of their anguish.

Business icons rip off millions of people to further engorge their bulging coffers. Despite their inhumanity and complete lack of conscience, they represent what appears to be a successful male paradigm, where immoral and even criminal ends justify the means.

Professional athletes, sometimes referred to as *"All-American"* — as if they represented the very best that the U.S. has to offer. We hear about them on the nightly news, throwing tantrums, taking illegal body building or performance enhancing drugs, and being charged with rape. Advertisers portray them as ultimate images of manhood, despite their obvious short-comings. And young people buy into that.

Politicians selling out to big business, contriving slurs and telling outright lies about their opponents, all for the accumulation of power.

Media journalists, once considered heroic bastions of truth, now prostituting their trade, focusing on the lowest common denominator of titillating gossip while foisting their own political bias on a public in desperate need for truth.

The results are apparent. Jails are overflowing. Wealthy businessmen violate the trust of innocent people. Politicians ignore the threat of pollution and global warming, even encouraging the populace to burn as much oil as they possibly can. Pornographers are treated as respectable businesspeople. Even religious leaders are now suspect, with thousands of charges of child molestations made against them and a Church dragging its feet in response.

This is the society that young people grow up in — a society without heroes, without myth, where virtues are so coupled with hypocrisy that they can no longer be held in esteem.

While many factors contribute to this, a central component is the degradation of what it means to be a man in relationship to the world. Men still carry a lot of power — but it is power that often lacks a viable moral compass.

The denial of cultural identity is akin to ripping out a person's conscience, taking away his name, firing him from his job, stealing his language, cutting him off from friends and family. Cultural identities, especially those of gender, need to be recognized for the role they play in people's lives. They need to be honored, but they also need to be *honorable*, while retaining a strong continuity with the past.

In short, they need to evolve.

Part of the problem stems from the growing rapidity of social change that started with the Industrial Revolution, when men traded their independence for the closed-in, repetitive conditions of the factory. Cut off from a respectful relationship with nature, they no longer performed work that varied with the seasons. They no longer worked side-by-side with their children to mentor them. This resulted in a cultural shock with on-going ramifications.

The development of technology has distracted us from this trauma by "making life easier," glossing over the broken status quo by adding benefits of convenience. Despite the continual advance of scientific and psychological progress (or maybe because of it?), we drift even further from knowing who we are in the depth of our being. We live in a sort of stasis, confused, frustrated, looking for something — without knowing what.

The purpose of this book is to remedy that situation. Our goal is to first recover and then reinstate a viable cultural identity for men.

***

We start by looking back into our Western heritage to find a broad, historically based foundation of male ethics that we can build on. We find exactly what we need in the well-articulated literature of medieval times — a comprehensive warrior code known as *chivalry*.

Chivalry was a code of principles or standards of behavior that reflected the values of the warrior class of European knights.

While this code was never officially defined into law, a vast amount of literature and poetry described it for posterity. Largely fictional characters of chivalry remain famous even today: King Arthur and his Knights of the Round Table: Lancelot, Gawain, Galahad, Perceval and Tristan. There are historical examples as well, including William Marshal, Bertrand du Guesclin, and King Richard Coeur de Lion.

4

As a warrior ethic, chivalry required truth, mercy to one's enemies, service to women, protection of the weak, and defense of the good — all encompassed by a sense of justice, loyalty, courtesy, humility, generosity, and brotherhood among the knightly caste.

These virtues were never effete, but sprang from a manly strength that was tempered by self-control. Thanks to chivalry, the self-disciplined knight was not only strong but congenial as well. Polite, caring, protective, even religious in the case of the Knights Templar and the Knights Hospitaler of St John. Above all, they were admirably masculine.

Through the influence of Arthurian tales, these ethics became codified, multifaceted and social. For the most part, both the Church and women approved.

This elegant code was largely disseminated by the literature of the High Middle Ages, stories shaped by Celtic legend, wandering troubadours, and Islamic influence transplanted by Crusader veterans.

Wealthy female sponsors, women like Marie de Champagne, eagerly used this genre to refine courtly behavior from its ale house origins, thus civilizing the ideals of their male audience. They successfully incorporated the newly formed concept of romantic love into tales of knightly heroism.

Priestly clerics, hoping to curb endemic violence, added their own Christianized veneer.

The result? A massive collection of stories, poems and songs that elevated and idealized proper behavior for the warrior caste, which eventually dispersed into the overall culture.

Chivalry enjoyed a powerful resurgence in England during the reign of Queen Victoria. Lord Tennyson's *Idylls of the King* sparked an Arthurian obsession which then inspired the works of the Pre-Raphaelite artists.

The most lasting expression of chivalry during this time was its influence in defining what it means to be a gentleman.

Although originally fashioned for aristocrats, the code filtered out to European society as a whole. One need not be a "gentleman" to behave like one.

The most popular tales were those of King Arthur and his knights, stories that dominated Europe for hundreds of years. The real Arthur was a Romano/Celtic hero who made his mark by effectively resisting Anglo-Saxon invaders. His legendary stories, Celtic in origin, were transplanted to the continent during the subsequent migrations of Celts to Brittany. Once in France, the stories gained a new and courtly dimension. Arthur, the somewhat obscure and mysterious Dark Age warlord, was thus transformed into an idealized king who was said to have conquered much of Europe.

The stories were filled with battles and pageantry, spiritual lessons and magic. They described a golden city called Camelot, where peace and justice reigned supreme. It was there that King Arthur formed the chivalrous order known as the Knights of the Round Table, where scores of heroic knights came together in a special companionship. Their adventures provided a never-ending surplus of Arthurian tales.

While these tales appealed to popular interest, the chivalrous behavior of the knights elevated the stories to a new level. The hero was not just the one who was strongest or cleverest, he was one who best exemplified certain moral ideals. This code of honor was a milestone in Western ethics that appealed to the warrior instincts of medieval men.

For our purposes, we find that chivalry provides the ethical foundation we need to guide us forward: distinctly Western, decidedly male, extolling the depth of a number of moral principles we still value today — principles evoking benefits for us all. What remains for us is to modify this code of behavior for the needs of the twenty-first century by progressively adding insights born from such sources as the Age of Enlightenment and modern psychology.

***

After years of studying Arthurian literature from a cultural perspective, I compiled the following principles into a new *Code of Chivalry* appropriate for our times. I call it the *Twelve Trusts*.

The Twelve Trusts
Upon my honor...

1. I will *develop my life* for the greater good.
2. I will *place character above riches, and concern for others* above personal wealth.
3. I will *never boast*, but cherish *humility* instead.
4. I will *speak the truth* at all times, and forever keep my word.
5. I will *defend* those who cannot defend themselves.
6. I will *honor and respect women*, and refute sexism in all its guises.
7. I will *uphold justice* by being fair to all.
8. I will be *faithful in love* and *loyal* in friendship.
9. I will *abhor scandal and gossip* — neither partake nor delight in them.
10. I will be *generous* to the poor and to those who need help.
11. I will *forgive* when asked, that my own mistakes will be forgiven.
12. I will *live my life with courtesy and honor* from this day forward.

By adhering to the Twelve Trusts, I swear to partake in the living *Quest* in everything I do.

These tenets will be used throughout this book as topics for discussion. The result will be an updated ethic for men called **Chivalry-Now**.

***

You might ask at this point: *who are you to write about such things?*

Let me state right up front, as clearly as I can, that I am by no means some paradigm of virtue for others to emulate. I have merely thought long and hard about these issues in the light of my own experience and the experiences of those around me, and fell sway to their inspiration.

My interest in the subject stems from an early age. As a child I led a sheltered life with few, if any, positive male role models. This started me off on a life-long quest to learn exactly what it means to be a man.

For well over 20 years I obsessively indulged myself with training in the martial arts. This put me in touch with the warrior spirit, not as a student or disciple, but as a son in search of his father's voice that lay hidden in the development of self-control.

While working in social services, I interviewed hundreds of men and women who were in need of help. Listening to their stories, decisions and the values they expressed, I became convinced that their problems extended well beyond food, clothing and shelter. Many of them seemed confused by the contradictions and lack of direction of their own culture. Men especially seemed to have no sure concept of what it means to be a man. It was their confusion, inner grief, and lack of personal discipline that caused them to fail their wives, families, their community — and ultimately themselves. Nothing in the culture seemed to teach them anything different.

Last but not least in my quest for understanding, I have witnessed the intrinsic beauty of the chivalrous life in fact and in fiction, and it has moved me deeply. It has acquainted me with my own deficiencies, and influenced my own life in no small measure of personal change.

Chivalry has taught me that many of our problems stem from a cultural inheritance that is fragmented, scattered, and often contradictory, and we can improve things if we have a mind to do so.

We start by improving ourselves, you and me. Our culture begins to regenerate only through our own efforts. I hope you welcome the challenge as much as I have. As with any quest, its reward comes in direct proportion to the effort put into it.

Chapter 1

Chivalry

When most people hear the word *chivalry*, one of two popular images come to mind: knights in shining armor perched on powerful steeds, or gentlemen opening doors for ladies.

They might not understand how chivalry once served as a surprisingly comprehensive ethic, a seamless tapestry of integrated ideals, beautifully portrayed in the literature of the High Middle Ages. This behavioral code was not formulated for women or children or pious clerics, but for elite warriors, hardened knights who considered its moral directives more of a privilege than responsibility. With chivalry as their guide, they acted mercifully as well as justly. They defended the weak, served and honored women, and acted courteously toward all.

The ethics of chivalry were not imposed from the outside. They were not the result of some law or religious demand. They were a collection of ideals that originated within men themselves. Through chivalry, aspiring knights recognized their own personal value as men of honor and acted accordingly. They viscerally recognized the importance of being a man of strength, truth and compassion. The culture, in turn, validated and supported this claim.

Although the social morality of the Middle Ages was sorely inadequate by today's standards, chivalry stood out as a notable high point in Western history. That it arose from its own accord in the midst of medieval brutality warrants our close inspection.

***

As a powerful example of male ethics, historically-based chivalry provides the cultural precursor of precepts we need today, when young men and old contend with a world where ethics have been degraded by political expediency, unscrupulous marketing, and the addictive qualities of its entertainment industry.

That being said, we find ourselves contending with the appropriateness of something as simple as politely opening doors for women. How do we justify such courtesies in light of feminist reprisals?

The world we live in bombards us with pseudo-cultural messages that contradict chivalry's values, clichés like: *nothing matters but the bottom line; take care of number one; it's not my problem; winning is everything; every man for himself; you have to love yourself before you can love someone else.*

As familiar maxims, such words promise much with their decisive tone. What they deliver is a social vision that fails to consider our deepest values. They produce a morality in conflict with itself, where time-honored strivings are replaced by a bland follower mentality that only serves to deaden the soul.

Our commercialized society seems to support the rise of feminism. But does it do this because it cares for the good of women? Or is it riding a wave of opinion in order to capitalize on it? Notice how it fails to support male issues by interjecting scorn and roadblocks. Men are portrayed on television programs and commercials as mindless, empty shells, preoccupied with sex, ego gratification or the trappings of power. Constantly feeding our society with such images only propagates them as fact.

This commercialized mindset has robbed us of our vitality, our purpose and meaning. It is the enemy within that assails us constantly.

To effectively combat this, we need to recognize its source. Simply put, the lack of a cultural definition of what it means to be a man throws everything off balance.

Chivalry once provided this understanding with an effective

code of belief and behavior. In the midst of a powerful Victorian resurgence, however, chivalry found itself contending with an economic challenge that would spell its eventual demise. The *Industrial Revolution*. All of a sudden, the cultural means of transmitting male values from father to son was crushed.

It was the coming of the factory and the subsequent migration to the city that separated boys from the natural mentoring of their fathers, grandfathers, uncles, and neighbors. No longer did they learn the expectations of manhood first-hand. They were abandoned to learn fundamental principles on their own. This cultural shift was brutally traumatic to those first generations. Make no mistake, we are victimized by the results even today.

In previous eras, the survival needs of family and tribe determined what characteristics were valued in men. The purpose of a culture was to create worthy citizens: strong providers and protectors, good fathers, dedicated husbands, honest brokers, men who upheld the values that communities esteemed.

This cultural flow was replaced by the repressive "work ethic" of the factory, with fathers and husbands regimentally disappearing for the most productive hours of the day. When they returned, exhausted, it was not with a brace of killed game or produce in hand, the actual fruit of their skill and labor, but with a paycheck that quickly went to paying bills.

Most of the time their hands were empty, with nothing to show for their labor at all.

A fundamental dynamic between father and son was broken, the very dynamic that provided a sense of connection, identity and pride. In short order, masculine ideals became more and more detached from family interactions. Soon they were only glimpsed from a receding shore, their depth of meaning swiftly forgotten.

When life is relegated to the repetition of the assembly-line or office for eight or ten hours a day, with home life an afterthought, something inside us dies an ignoble death — something essential that we still mourn, bitterly at times, yet scarcely recollect.

Because of this, our common morality became confused, superficial, conflicted, and sometimes even expendable. Our natural understanding of right and wrong could no longer enjoy the structure and moral nourishment that our culture used to provide. Traditional interactions with families and friends that once supported our highest inclinations have dissipated, replaced by the same expediency that rules the factory or corporation. If there is a faster, more economical way to get things done, do it. If something gets lost in the process, it becomes an acceptable risk. The only thing that counts is profit.

But what if one of the things we lose defines our basic humanity? Conveyor-belt ethics cannot replace the complexity that once defined men as people, intrinsically valuable to their families and friends. The resulting emptiness is a direct cause of the pervasive male frustration we see today, contributing to all our long-term and short-term problems.

On the bright side, identifying the cause of our problems is the first step to repairing them, which is the noble intention of this book.

Returning an updated version of chivalry to our culture will reestablish a proper focus in men's lives. By encouraging more informed and logical choices, men will do their natural part, alongside women, in transforming the world into a better place to live.

Chapter 2

"Upon My Honor..."

What exactly did chivalry promote as a male ethic?

Honesty, generosity, loyalty, justice, humility, the advocacy of what is right and good, the avoidance of slander, defense of women's rights, and a special delight for those willing to try it, romantic love. These attributes were recognized as the most admirable qualities of real men.

They still are, although we scarcely give them their honorable due.

Our new vision of chivalry, what we call *Chivalry-Now*, derives its authority from the same principles as its medieval counterpart. It projects a vision that has evolved from its medieval roots to be appropriate for today's needs.

Imagine a business ethic based on fairness, compassion and good will, rather than manipulative, amoral commercialism. Imagine a popular support for equality, where women and minorities no longer have to fight for equal rights. Imagine a citizenry of men who so cherish what is good that the crime rate plummets. How about truth in politics, and leaders chosen for their real intelligence and good will? Marriages built on equal partnerships, with men fulfilling their spousal and parental responsibilities? Imagine a news media more concerned with truth than entertainment. Imagine the inspiration of a new slate of ethics rippling throughout entire populations, lowering tensions across the globe.

This illustrates some of the grand possibilities that Chivalry-Now hopes to foster. It comprises the dream of the new *knight-errant*.

***

Medieval chivalry was produced by a world perspective that was radically different from ours. Some of its beliefs and behaviors are now completely inappropriate, such as duels, trial by combat, and undeserved privileges of the aristocracy. While medieval chivalry held ladies in high esteem, it never recognized their full potential as human beings. In other words, it reflected the feudal values of the world it came from, and would not be acceptable to modern society.

To discover what potential chivalry holds for us today, we need to project what it would be like if it had survived and evolved with the times. What would it be like if it incorporated some of the liberating ideas of the Age of Enlightenment, like freedom, democracy, and equality? How would psychology have influenced it? Science? World politics? And what about the dark specters of modern warfare and environmental poisoning?

Chivalry would do its best to preserve its core ideals, according to the knowledge and experience of the times. It would constantly have to "come of age," adjusting to reality in order to serve as a viable dynamic. Its ideals would continue to influence the way we see things, our everyday choices, and our relationships.

Chivalry-Now is different from its glorious but dated predecessor. It takes the powerful spirit and ideals of that knightly ethic and presents them with new applicability. Not a soft-pedaling rearrangement of details, trying to fit what we have already, but a fresh, new vision that safeguards its original depth and relevance.

***

The Twelve Trusts — Our Structural Beginning
Upon my honor...

1. I will *develop my life* for the greater good.
2. I will *place character above riches, and concern for others* above personal wealth.
3. I will *never boast,* but cherish *humility* instead.
4. I will *speak the truth* at all times, and forever keep my word.
5. I will *defend* those who cannot defend themselves.
6. I will *honor and respect women,* and refute sexism in all its guises.
7. I will *uphold justice* by being fair to all.
8. I will be *faithful in love* and *loyal* in friendship.
9. I will *abhor scandal and gossip* — neither partake nor delight in them.
10. I will be *generous* to the poor and to those who need help.
11. I will *forgive* when asked, that my own mistakes will be forgiven.
12. I will *live my life with courtesy and honor* from this day forward.

By adhering to the Twelve Trusts, I swear to partake in the living Quest in everything I do.

The Twelve Trusts furnish those who are interested in Chivalry-Now with a basic code of ethics to build upon. Using them as a pocket guide, we begin our quest by focusing on the introductory words: *Upon my Honor...* Just like the old, this is where our new chivalry begins.

I don't recall the first time I heard the word *honor* and intuited what it meant, or felt confident using the term. Like most men, however, I knew that it referenced something inside me, inside us all, that was irreproachably honest and trustworthy, and could be called upon when needed. We all know what it means when we say "I give you my word." It holds us to a higher standard that originates nowhere but in ourselves. It is life transforming, if only for a moment. It draws our reality into something deeply authentic, something accountable to... *what?*

The essence of honor points to standards we intuitively believe in, yet often neglect during our daily routine.

Here we find our path to personal authenticity, the spiritual affirmation of who we are in thought, word and deed. As men of honor, we see the world differently, we behave differently. This impetus comes as much from ourselves as from the expectations of others. It refers to the integrity that defines us.

That being said, the word honor is often used with superficial understanding of what it really means. People often confuse it with *pride*.

When Chivalry-Now refers to honor, it does not refer to a concept of pride that wraps itself in ego and lends itself to conceit. It refers to a *personal proficiency of chivalric principles*. One might consider it a *reputation for moral integrity* — but it is more than that. It is a commitment to right action, a commitment so strong that it shapes a person's consciousness accordingly. It is a dedication of self to something greater than oneself, not to some group or person, but to grand ideals. Expressing a fusion of the soul with chivalric ideals, it provides the ethical foundation of manliness.

A man of honor is someone who can be trusted: honest, well-intentioned, strong, committed to what is good. He is an oasis in a desert wasteland, worthy of praise, yet unmoved by flattery. He owns the inner qualities of the truest hero.

His concern with reputation extends only as a measurement of his commitment. It is difficult to perceive a man as honorable who willfully subverts his reputation — and yet we see it every day. Hardened criminals care little about their moral image, while the worst of our politicians feel they can dissemble truth with impunity.

When pride encourages or enhances moral commitment, it serves us well. We call this *human-pride*, an inner motivation to do the right thing, not for show or credit, but out of respect for our common humanity. In stark contrast is *ego-pride*, in which image and reputation becomes an end unto itself.

Honor begins with *truth*, and quickly extends itself to *personal integrity*. The honorable man is concerned not only for his own *well-being*, but for that of others as well. One cannot separate honor from action and relationship.

To clarify this idea, let us examine what honor *is not*:

- There is no honor in boasting or belittling other people.
- There is no honor in dulling one's mind and judgment with alcohol or drugs. Doing so detracts from completeness and clarity of mind.
- There is no honor in harming innocent people, in victimizing or controlling women, or placing profit ahead of compassion.
- There is no honor in telling people lies or delighting in gossip and slander.
- There is no honor in smearing an opponent, political or otherwise, with false allegations.
- There is no honor in cheating or breaking promises.
- There is no honor in complacency in the face of injustice, especially when opportunity calls for bold action.
- There is no honor in winning when it compromises the integrity of your soul.
- There is no honor in being false concerning matters of love.

In the eyes of chivalry, only the man of honor is really a man — and that goes for Chivalry-Now as well. Only in the proper functioning of our souls do we find the well-spring of truth, beauty and human value that ultimately defines us — and sets us free.

Chapter 3

The Inner Source of Chivalry-Now

One of the fundamental premises of this book is that chivalry's appeal, its song, its very essence, originates not from outside us, but from the distinct commonality of men's souls. It is who we are when moments of authenticity strike. Because we feel this affirmation so directly in ourselves, we can be sure that we have found the definition of manhood we are looking for.

The prevalence of crime, overcrowded prisons, violence against women, dysfunctional families, broken marriages, fathers who cannot relate to their children, unethical business practices and ethically challenged CEOs, preachers who subvert their faith for profit, political leaders who betray the interests of their nation for twelve pieces of silver — all these and more, originate from our failure to propagate healthy male virtues in a world where unscrupulous men still hold an inordinate amount of power.

Without a viable template of what it means to be a man, we end up learning from what is available, images that are incomplete, broken, or completely dysfunctional. We learn from characters provided by the entertainment industry: cowboys, con-men, spies and assassins, thieves and organized crime bosses. People like Al Capone and Jesse James, and Bonnie and Clyde are still regarded as popular heroes. Some of us find strange reassurance in the neurotic complexity of the anti-hero — someone we can identify with, without being challenged to improve.

But to what end?

I am convinced that the infamous propensity of many men to exhibit poor communication is founded by an internal disconnect with their core values. Perhaps their all too common answer to questions that matter, "I don't know," expresses more truth than evasion. Maybe they *don't know* because their powers of discernment are broken, or they are too focused on the opinions of others, ignoring the truer source of value that comes from within.

***

In quiet moments you can almost hear it. Not the proverbial still, small voice. More like a grumble of discontent, a demeaning undercurrent you cannot escape from.

Like the ghostly appearance of Hamlet's father, it laments the course of fratricide that condemns it to endless, shackled wandering.

Occasionally these introspective moments become disconcerting. You feel thwarted everywhere you look, without a hint of recourse. Inexplicable anger rises in your chest, deep-seated frustration, like labor pains of self-birth that are constantly thwarted.

It is like knowing that you have been compelled to live someone else's life and there is nothing you can do to change it.

You sense that the world has betrayed you right from the start. You were born too late or too early to fit in with your surroundings. This lack of validation is total. You search for the possibility that something better might exist, or should exist, or could, if things were only different. Complacency and routine prick your conscience with insignificance. You know you were born for something greater. Even though it was denied you, or stolen at an early age, it still haunts your conscience with the possibility of a fulfilling life.

It tells you that you are different from what people see. There exists in you an imprisoned hero, unfulfilled, unappreciated, straining for liberation.

Let us call him your *knight-errant,* your intuitive *man of chivalry.*

***

What is a *knight-errant?*
Historically, it referred to a medieval knight so inspired by chivalry that he wandered about the countryside looking for adventure. The word errant, or *errantry,* can also refer to straying from the norm, a reference to detachment and individuality.

Chivalry-Now recognizes today's knight-errant as a man who has found his moral center, lives by it with integrity, and views the challenges of life for the adventures that they are. The knight-errant expresses the purpose and meaning of his ideals in everything he does, while striving to make the world a better place. He does not do this for reward or recognition, but because of who he is. Not perfect. Just a man doing his best.

This concept of the knight-errant is an attractive and reachable goal for today's man of chivalry, but should not be taken lightly. It involves a solemn, honor-bound commitment to one's ideals.

***

Chivalry owns a timeless appeal despite its Dark Age origins. The majority of women agree with this, despite the expectations of some to the contrary.

Why? Perhaps it is chivalry's inherent link to simple qualities that humanize us, like truth, courtesy, cooperative relationships, and helping those in need. Perhaps it is those finer aspects of the *warrior spirit* that chivalry sprang from: strength, honor, loyalty, self-discipline, the willingness to sacrifice one's life for a good cause.

Or perhaps it is the *aura of completeness* that a positive code of ethics naturally exudes.

We naturally expect the chivalrous man to be more refined, genuine and trustworthy — someone you can count on to do the right thing. Such expectations point to an instinctive admiration for solid male qualities. Chivalrous men make better friends and husbands, fathers and co-workers, soldiers and political leaders. Their steady values make sense, and are not dependent upon pop-psychology or the latest trend. They are grounded in something deeply rooted in the centuries, something we sense as our birthright — even as the world denies us.

Chivalry is the most succinct cultural and historical expression of male ethics in the West. In the East, the Japanese warrior code of Bushido reflects a time-honored variation as well. In other places of the world, where such ethics might not be called by formal names like chivalry or Bushido, they can still be found in the warrior-spirit of honorable men.

Part of the reason we find chivalry so appealing is that it reflects principles that are necessary not only for the good of men, but for the completeness of the human race — as necessary as female qualities that daily support humanity's survival.

The message is simple. Each gender either contributes to the well-being of our species, or detracts from it by not doing its part.

Male ethics is necessary to this process because its loss results in broken, incomplete men who wallow in frustration and gravitate toward anti-social behavior that effects everyone.

Chapter 4

"I will Develop my Life…"

Trust #1:
I will Develop my life for the greater good.

Like most young men, my journey from childhood to adolescence sparked a strong desire to become more than who I was.

Lacking the normal introductions, I had no interest in sports like most boys. I had no interest in school either — no interest in anything other than the escapism of comic books and sketching, which occupied most of my free time.

Then, one day, I was pushed aside by a schoolyard bully. No surprise there. I was third shortest in my class, skinny, timid and not athletic. A bully magnet — and I knew it.

On this particular occasion, however, the way he bullied me left an indelible mark. Why? Because he scarcely looked at me, as if I were too insignificant to even acknowledge.

Angry and insulted, I tried to retaliate by ineffectively tackling his legs to bring him down. He just looked at me, annoyed by the distraction, and shook me away.

I felt like less than nothing.

I do not relate this looking for sympathy. I grew to be a head taller than the bully, and my long involvement with the martial arts freed me from such worries again.

The point I am making is that I learned from this incident, and others like it, to take control over my life and change things for the better. No one was going to do that for me.

Studying non-classical kung-fu, for example, I not only learned my craft, I discovered ways of punching harder than anyone I knew, and developed speed of attack that astounded even me.

The lesson I learned, which applied to all aspects of my life, was this: if I want to be free, if I want to truly be myself as a person, I had to shape and build my own potential. I had to develop skills and talents and intellect in order to live confidently in the world, discover who I am, and direct my life accordingly.

This only scratches the surface of what chivalric self-development is all about. The effort produces a moral and ethical imperative as well — the imperative of personal integrity. Without the values it generates, we are incomplete, our lives unfulfilled.

Having a humble or not so humble background should not dissuade us. Our childhood interests should not either. My whimsical pencil sketching eventually produced drawings that rivaled photographs in detail. Comic book reading led to storytelling which progressed to professional writing. My peculiar approach to martial arts training, as an independent explorer, resulted in a liberation of mind and spirit that extended to all areas of my life. Combining all this with a love for philosophy and Arthurian literature, along with years administering welfare policy, contributed to the discovery of Chivalry-Now.

We cannot enjoy a full, authentic life without taking strong efforts in developing the uniqueness of who we are and then extending that for the betterment of all.

***

In a personal sense, Chivalry-Now activates itself when the individual takes control of his life and dedicates his personal development for the greater good. Without this actualization of deeper self, asserted through discipline to training and commitment to practice, our true identities remain trapped and disconnected from their full potential.

When it comes to personal change, it is easy to be complacent, shrug our shoulders and say, "Life isn't so bad. Why change now? Life is too short. I'll just enjoy whatever tidbits come my way."

That might seem a viable direction. Keep in mind, however, that the apathy and neglect it produces completely undermines what being a man is all about. It makes cowards out of heroes, and sustains the ethical void that we all suffer from.

People who feel ambivalent about moral directives like those of chivalry often confuse complacency with contentment. While they may feel as if they are thinking for themselves, their partial and confused reasoning shows that they are not. They have become victims of the moral malaise that consumerism propagates, where happiness is equated with a new car, or the latest fashion, or losing weight. They have adopted the role of the consummate consumer, convinced that the *good life* should ask nothing of them other than their credit scores. While they might not condone suffering in the world, they do not lift a finger to change it.

Here we find the uncritical herd mentality, the same thoughtless complacency that allows corrupt politicians and preachers to flourish unchallenged. *Follow the crowd; don't make waves; vote for this reason and not for that; close your eyes and have faith in big government; reject government altogether.*

In this fashion we contribute to a disinterested democracy that languishes in commercialism like a drug addict — to the profit of someone else.

Freedom loses its substance as we sacrifice ourselves to meaningless routine, or alcohol, or drugs, or the television remote, or the Internet, or competing with our neighbors.

Chivalry-Now represents the antithesis of herd mentality. It encourages and inspires people to think for themselves and find truth on their own. Through inspiration, not compulsion, it liberates people from their own complacency, from values imposed on them by the propagation of indifference.

Remember. *The ideals we advocate are yours already.* They always have been. Chivalry-Now merely speaks the moral language that your heart understands. We make no claims that are not self-evident, and we do not seek followers. Indeed, we reject the *follower* mentality as completely missing the mark. Those whom we consider *Companions* are autonomous brothers and sisters of the quest, explorers all, who accept each other as friends and share ideas.

***

Medieval chivalry represents the heart and soul of what it means to be a man, and nothing has replaced it in a thousand years. It proclaimed the value of certain ideals that were not based on reward or punishment or external mandate, but on their own merit. This tapestry of values, rooted in the warrior spirit, was masculine to the core: practical yet idealistic, strong yet compassionate, powerful yet disciplined, a benefit to others as well as to oneself. Chivalry not only recognized what was virtuous in men, it described those virtues as the source of their identity. Men defined themselves by their beliefs.

From today's perspective, we tend to define ourselves by the opinions of others. When those opinions and the principles they are based on contradict each other, or lack significant depth, where do we turn to find answers? Another guru? Another New Age idea? Psychotherapy? Our insecurities tell us that we can't find answers for ourselves. But is that true? Is not the finding of those answers the very *quest* that makes us human?

In many respects, we face the same mythical journey as those early knights, and the warriors who preceded them. We refer to it as the *quest*, an untrodden path to self-discovery, self-empowerment, independence — and most important of them all, to bettering the world we live in. We become men only when we achieve a positive relationship with the world around us. As a builder of men, the natural expression of our nobility, Chivalry makes that possible.

Without this moral and spiritual connection — which should be our cultural inheritance — we are disconnected from who we really are. Our dreams are distorted. Our aspirations misdirected. Our roles confused. Our place in the scheme of things bewilderingly nonexistent. What remains is a voiceless discontent, a frustration that challenges the entire structure of our lives.

That is why chivalry retains such a powerful connection, a mixture of hope and conscience, rooted in our legitimate past and psychological being. Chivalry-Now gives birth to knight-errantry when pain and promise converge into action.

What Chivalry-Now asks is nothing more than a personal commitment to life. Only in commitment does a man find purpose and meaning, and freedom as well. This is where the energy and excitement of life come from.

The commitment must be freely given. It must reflect what is best inside us in order to be authentic. Anything less will fail, no matter how popular or profitable.

Shakespeare told us *"to thine own self be true."* Chivalry-Now asks nothing more, but insists on nothing less.

Self-development begins with the liberation of one's mind, the shedding of those obstacles given to us by family, teachers, friends, and the ever-indulgent media. It means questioning things — inherited values especially. It means searching with a clear eye for the truth behind reality, not just for now but for the rest of your life. The alternative is adopting the basic value system of someone else. If you feel any self worth, why should that person's values take precedence over your own?

We are conscious creatures in search of more consciousness, not less. But consciousness carries responsibilities. When we sacrifice our lives to consumerism or a misleading ideology, we reject the fullness of who we are, and the challenges we *need* to face.

We forget that our lives should make a difference before they end. A non-obsessive concern about tomorrow does not subtract from the experience of life, it helps perpetuate a better world for ourselves and future generations.

*****

Our culture fails us on many fronts.

When we sit a boy in front of the television or video-game for a significant part of the day, we do not impart the kind of heartfelt love and instruction that parents are meant to give. We are not nurturing him with a sense of family and community obligation by subjecting his mind to nonsensical sitcoms, cop shows, and commercials that say and do anything to manipulate his mind to sell a product.

As concerned parents, what can we expect children to learn from the entertainment media?

Honesty? You will find little of it in commercial marketing or in politics.

Loyalty? Not in business. Nothing counts but the bottom line.

Defending the weak? We have special interest groups for that. (Special interest groups, like environmentalists who have to contend with the clout of big business.)

Justice? Hard to find, no matter where you look.

The defeat of *sexism?* Despite significant gains made by women, the glass ceiling still exists, and pornography thrives.

Humility? How does that fit into a world that worships celebrity? Everything boils down to image.

Even the benign impulse of *generosity* has been tainted by false charities, exorbitant administrative costs and the lure of tax incentives.

Love? Little is expected from love today, beyond getting what you want from another person for as long as it lasts.

Contradictions are so prevalent and engrained that we scarcely see them. We have adapted instead, and then wonder where our feelings of discontent come from.

Communities ask nothing from us beyond paying taxes and obeying the law (even those requirements are flexible for some). No heart. No soul. No belonging. No ethical roots. It is all about profit and image. Our grand democracy draws few participants at town meetings. Even the simple act of voting is ignored by many. In the 2000 U.S. presidential election, only 51% of the voters turned out, showing a constant decline from the 65% level in 1960. That this increased in 2008 to 62% shows a hopeful trend.

In stark contrast, the young knight of the Middle Ages faced a very different world — harsher, yes, but more in touch with human nature. Justice was something to consider with every decision he made. His world demanded it. Heroism was not about throwing a ball or posing in front of a camera. It was putting one's life on the line for others.

Things were more real, more grounded in life's essentials, less plagued by instant illusions. The interconnectedness of life in nature and society was more evident in daily routines. Foul weather had a direct and meaningful impact. The mutual bond between lord and vassal often meant the difference between life and death.

Simple pleasures were highly esteemed. Entertainment was a rare and much appreciated diversion, not a steady flow of commercial attractions dominating significant parts of every day.

Today's need for constant entertainment detracts from our sense of authenticity. We search desperately for the feeling of being alive, while everything we touch numbs our ability to experience it.

***

We all recognize youth as a time for growth and self-development. But it does not end there. Chivalry-Now talks about the liberation that comes from exploring the ongoing, never-ending process of personal growth. Self-development is more than learning facts and honing skills. It involves character building as well. Chivalry is not a set of rules to follow. It is who we are. That makes our goal the same as the knight-errant: preparing ourselves for the challenges of life and for the greater good. This development encompasses the entire person: physical, intellectual, spiritual. Anything less detracts from who we are.

Today's knight-errant is called to develop his full potential.

He should be as strong and flexible as his health and his body allows so that he can respond to injustice.

He should have a liberal appreciation of the complexity of life and all its challenges and not be restrained by ideology.

He should hone his awareness of meaning and dedication to truth, in order to fully approach the spiritual dimensions of life.

Does this bar a fellow with cognitive disabilities, or some physical impairment? Not at all. People with disabilities often reach more of their full potential than the unimpaired, which puts them ahead in the personal game of life.

Self-development is not about who we are in relationship to the world, but who we can be. It is not a comparison of one person with another, but a comparison with our full potential.

We are men in our minds and bodies and spirit, or we are not men at all. There are no halfway measures, just different levels of achievement, depending on ability.

Chapter 5

"Character above Riches ..."

Trust #2: I will place character above riches, and concern for others above personal wealth.

When we say a person has *character* certain qualities come to mind. Chief among them are honesty, strength, fearlessness, moral integrity and independence of thought. Such qualities contribute to what chivalry describes as a noble personality, the laudable attribute of a true knight.

We attain a measure of this nobility when we reclaim our natural inheritance as men. The rest comes from living our lives accordingly.

Character is a state of mind as well as a product of will.

Strength of character reflects more of a steadfast intelligence than unwavering resolve. Too often we see men of resolve do stupid things and then fail to take a better course due to a prideful inability to admit mistakes. We see this in politics with disastrous results, not the least of which was the Iraq War.

Politicians are convinced that voters respect even ignorant resolve over someone who changes his mind as he continues to grow. Perhaps they are right. Open minded people are then labeled as wafflers, and are derided for being weak or inconsistent. This conclusion, pervasive as it seems, comes from a shallow understanding of the word resolve, which politicians tend to buy into. Resolve suggests character, even by itself. Voters naturally trust people who exhibit character. Their line of reasoning unfortunately seems to end there. As in most things, when you cling to cheap substitutes of profound moral principles, it leads to disaster.

The *fearless* quality of the noble character also tends to be misinterpreted. Noble fearlessness means standing up for one's principles even when it is not advantageous to do so. This takes courage and moral integrity — attributes we rarely see in politics or the business world or just about anywhere. Imitators fail to incorporate the moral dimension. They replace it with a reckless "I don't care as long as I get what I want" attitude, often loud and obnoxious, a caricature of manliness that reflects poorly on us all.

Moral integrity and independence of thought are inseparable aspects of moral character. Moral integrity without independent thought is little more than blind stubbornness. Independence without morality disconnects itself from the core of who we are as men.

Character denotes a high level of *self-discipline*. Anyone can do what is right now and then, especially when someone is watching. It is a matter of choice. The man of character makes the right choices more consistently, without question or need for reward. He looks to his own conscience.

Perhaps self-discipline is not the right term. *Self-mastery* is better.

The man of character, the man of chivalry, the masculine ideal we are conjuring, exerts a high level of control or mastery over who he is, his habits, his courteous behavior, his fears. Such mastery automatically differentiates him from people who succumb to license or unchallenged neuroses. It makes him more real, more genuinely human.

In Victorian times, there was often a cold air of superiority that accompanied self-disciplined behavior, especially among those of the upper class. We saw some of this in medieval times as well. Chivalry-*then* contributed to class distinctions and privileges.

In contrast, Chivalry-*Now* has thankfully evolved. It recognizes itself as a male expression of humane behavior that incorporates the best of humanity in its full dimension. This includes the power of reason and intellect, but also instinct and emotion. It points to a depth of *personal freedom*, while simultaneously pointing to *personal commitment*, recognizing the relationship between the two. Only a free person is capable of making a free and therefore genuine commitment.

The man of character is not locked into a preconceived image. He is as flexible as life makes him. While he takes life seriously, he can be comical as well. Steadfast beliefs do not eliminate spontaneity. Self-control does not prevent tears when appropriate, or laughter, occasional foolishness, or empathy — the whole gamut of life experiences that make us human.

What it does do is make him dependable and trustworthy, a dedicated husband, father, advocate, and friend.

***

There are barriers and distractions that interfere with the development of character.

The lure of riches, obsession with money, the urge to accumulate power or material possessions, have always clashed with the kind of morality and freedom that Chivalry-Now advocates.

In the Gospels, Jesus expressed this clearly: *"What profits a man to gain all the world but lose his soul?"* Jesus also warned, in no uncertain terms, about the rich man who barred himself from the Kingdom of Heaven because of his love of money.

Other religious and philosophical giants echo this sentiment. Buddha placed no stock in riches, preferring the *Middle Course*. Lao Tzu described the sage king as bringing peace to the land by claiming nothing.

While these admonitions have long been clear, they contend with a very different message which has become the heartbeat of our times: *money is everything.*

We are told that "the poor will inherit the earth," but we see the opposite everywhere we look. Even as the Ten Commandments tell us not to covet what others have, we are told that the spice of life is just the opposite.

This illustrates the sharp dichotomy in our values. We try to balance both sides, hoping to reap spiritual and material benefits at the same time. But we cannot balance values that contradict each other. The result is nothing less than a weakening of our moral standards.

Moral contradictions undercut our vision of the world because they undercut who we are. They teach us to embrace two conflicting sets of values, which ruins our capacity for moral discernment.

It is no wonder we prefer distractions.

It is no wonder that we prefer to follow the crowd or some charismatic leader, and let others do the thinking for us. The trouble is, both leader and crowd fall victim to the same dilemma we do.

We are told to love other people as ourselves, even as the prevailing consensus tells us to think only of *number one*. The so called Golden Rule, *Do unto others as you would have them do unto you*, that we enshrine as our foundation of morality, becomes easily set aside for reasons of profit or power.

There are preachers who shamelessly teach a theology of greed, despite the Bible's repeated condemnation against it.

Even many who reject "cash now theology" still base their religious teaching on reward and punishment, rather than respect for moral principles. The message of selfishness permeates everything.

The only way to rise above this is through the development of our own personal character. A man who respects truth, who is steadfast in his commitments and holds deep compassion for others, is not swayed by trends, half-baked ideas or moral contradictions. He sees things as they are and acts accordingly.

The second of the Twelve Trusts spells this out clearly.

I will place character above riches, and concern for others above personal wealth.

This is not a platitude. It is a requirement of our moral nature. It determines who we are and what we believe. It removes the dilemma of serving two masters, to which so many of us succumb.

We need to place people first in our lives, which is the essence of the Golden Rule.

***

The subject of character runs deeper than how we act or what we believe. It strikes the very core of our being.

Oscar Wilde once noted: *"Most people are other people. Their thoughts are someone else's opinions, their lives a mimicry, their passions a quotation."*

The building of one's character is nothing less than claiming possession of one's soul.

If we accept what others have made of us, and never strike out on our own, who are we? Indoctrinated salesmen shaped by the product we sell, or someone else's product?

Here we learn Chivalry-Now's first battle cry to action: *Build thyself.*

If we do not, others will do the work for us, according to their own haphazard design.

***

The quest to find authenticity is never simple. The world overflows with *distractions*, each vying for our attention.

It is obvious how alcohol and drug abuse divert us from the responsibilities of living, but television and football games often do the same on a different level.

The fruits of competition distract us from how we are hurting people or ruining the environment that sustains us. How can we sufficiently care for others when all we think about is winning?

Endless party bickering and scandal mongering distract political leaders from the decisions that desperately need to be made. Parties insist on fighting each other rather than working cooperatively. They feel comfortable doing this reassured that we are too distracted to notice or care.

We can be so distracted by our ambitions for our children's future that we fail to see or downplay their present needs. Soccer practice, piano and dance lessons, hanging out at the mall, wearing the latest fashion sneakers — what do all these distractions contribute as we plot their future? What are we teaching when we hand them off to the Internet to learn about life?

In dealing with social issues, we distract ourselves into complacency by supporting ineffective efforts to remedy them. Supporting costly treatment centers, endless therapy, welfare benefits, more police, more judges, and more prisons, may make us feel as if we are doing something, but the root causes remain untouched. The truth is, we will never end social problems by finding better ways to handle them. That halfway approach stops us from taking the problems seriously. For real solutions, we have to go to the source, to what generates those problems in our society. That is what needs to be changed.

Some years ago a novel idea hit the social services arena: *Prevention.* Instead of treating the cause, we took measures to prevent children from getting into trouble in a slightly different way.

How? Not by changing the root problems of their environment, or giving them something to believe in, but by means we are more familiar with. By *distracting them,* of course.

This well-meaning idea completely misplaced its focus. To be really effective, we need something more like *pre-prevention.* We need to eliminate, as far as possible, the problems that plague society at their source. Protecting the chosen few by putting them here instead of there only distracts us from bringing about serious change.

We do not need another distraction from doing what we have to do. As a society, it is time we grow up. We have to take away the glamour of doing what is wrong. We have to stop rewarding anti-social behavior. We have to develop a culture that is more humane. We have to start with the choices we make every day, and not allow ourselves to be distracted from the truth. As a people, we need the moral integrity to withdraw our support of what is wrong, no matter how passive it is. We need to morally refuse to profit from anything that hurts people. We need to reject and oppose the mindset that tries to distract us from, and so protect, the source of our problems.

Band-aid solutions to social infections only make things worse. The war on drugs cannot compete with a smirky acceptance of alcohol intoxication. The message is too arbitrary. We preach about standards of integrity and fair play in business and sports, and then lionize those who bend the rules and outright cheat to get ahead. With utmost hypocrisy, television news and panel discussions occasionally criticize their own sleazy coverage of scandal and celebrities, and then continue doing it just the same. A little conscience by itself does not get us where we need to go.

Until we consistently choose the high road, we will never serve as positive role models to our children.

***

Today's knight-errant places his own noble character, along with concern for others, before and above the acquisition of wealth or fame. Without that solid foundation, the ideals of chivalry have no proper footing. It becomes impossible to lead an honorable life, no matter how inoffensive his actions seem.

In that respect, the true knight-errant stands on his own ground. He belongs to a different realm, a kingdom fashioned by his soul's requirements. This is where honor originates — in the vision of high ideals applied to the practicality of the moment. It requires strength of character, the kind of strength that transcends the physical.

Acquiring this nobility is our birthright as men. It is our reach for authenticity.

The knight-errant calls for us to join him.

Chapter 6

"Never Boast, but Cherish Humility..."

Trust # 3: I will never boast, but cherish humility instead.

Humility is no longer thought of as the esteemed virtue that it was a thousand years ago. It contradicts the feel-good, be assertive, it's *all-about-me* attitude of today's pop-psychology.

Although boastfulness and conceit are sometimes considered poor taste, they gain more ascendancy every day. *Assertiveness training* helps us to walk the razor's edge, but completely disregards humility as something of value.

I remember a young couple who bragged to me once about how their *arrogance* (their word) helped them on job interviews. I was so taken back, I didn't know what to say. Arrogance worked and was therefore considered good. This utilitarian vision of the world is what we are up against. In order to properly separate the good from the bad, we will discuss the differences between *human-pride* and *ego-pride* later in this chapter.

Humility seems at odds with the prevailing wisdom of the marketplace: "You have to toot your own horn, sell yourself, show your best side at all times, fake it if you have to." This is reinforced by a steady flow of commercials: *"All eyes will be on you in these summer fashions. There's a new man in town. Why not drive a huge, completely unnecessary, gas guzzling vehicle? Think of the statement you'll make." (Yes indeed. Think of the statement.)*

These messages are not heard in a vacuum. They run contrary to long-held moral refrains that still echo in our psyche. The resulting conflict not only contributes to moral confusion, it promotes a disinterest in knowing what is really good, and makes what is not into something acceptable.

To understand why Chivalry-Now retains humility as an essential part of its code, we need to determine its place and value.

***

If we imagine the principles of chivalry to be individual stones comprising a castle wall, with honor as their connecting mortar, then humility provides the cornerstone. The loss of one stone may ruin the integrity of that wall, but without its cornerstone, the wall would never have been built.

We tend to think of humility as nothing more than a quaint "modesty of character" that has no purpose in today's graceless world. This shows how little we understand what humility is, and how it contributes something priceless to our quest.

For one thing, it provides a mindset more capable of confronting truth. It allows us to see our place in the universe for what it is by circumventing the clutter of ego-based delusions. We do not have to look at the world through the calculating lens of ego. We can look directly, without having to bend everything to our will.

Humility upholds other principles as well.

It graces the knight-errant with purity of intent, self-control, and a propensity for reason, which ego tends to disavow. It lends authenticity to courteous behavior. Justice and mercy come naturally to a humble man, richly adding to his character.

Humility removes the attraction of scandal and gossip, and helps us appreciate other people by allowing us to see them for who they are.

***

It is easier than most people think to justify the need for humility in our lives: the truth is, we have *good reason* to be humble.

We all make mistakes. Our perceptions and understandings are limited. No matter how much money we have or power we accumulate, none of that defines us. When ego defines us, we end up becoming smaller people, no matter how large we project our images. Our bodies are subject to nature, the same as beasts in the field. We age; we suffer; we die. True humility should therefore be seen as an attitude grounded in fact. It embraces the reality of who we are as human beings, limited and faulty, but striving to do our best.

***

The following examples come from people I have known who had profound influence on my life. For the reader to appreciate them, I must first share some of my own background.

During my early years, I was one of those boys who completely lacked a positive male role model. For the most part, my life was very solitary, with few social opportunities to learn from. My limited vision of the world was one of loneliness, fear, and insecurity. I was one of those quiet, nondescript children who slip through the cracks unnoticed.

Around the age of eleven I met a fellow who lived next door to my sister. His name was Hal, an art teacher by trade, and a father of three. My interest in sketching formed an immediate connection, at least in my mind. In his mind the connection must have seemed very slim. My sketching at the time focused on elephants and super-heroes.

Hal was easy to admire. Of Swedish descent, he was a tall, strong, hard-working, and considerate family-man who had a great sense of humor.

With all these fine qualities, he never acted superior or overbearing. Outgoing? Yes, but never offensive. He respected people's opinions and he was fun to be with. I envied his children who were younger than I was, too young to appreciate their good fortune.

He was the first man who was pleasant, sober, and acknowledged my existence. He quickly became my hero.

It was not that we spent much time together. Nevertheless, each quality moment taught me something special. My previous experience with adult men was more wounding than supportive. From an early age I knew that I did not want to be like them, angry or controlling or broodingly standoffish. Hal opened my eyes to wonderful alternatives.

He taught me through example that you do not have to fit any sort of contrived, belligerent stereotype to be a man. Quite the opposite. Like a Renaissance man, he had a wide variety of skills and interests, chosen by no one but himself.

He was not afraid to get his hands dirty in the yard. I once saw him cutting tall grass using the wide, curving strokes of an antiquated sickle. He was interested in religion, art and theater, especially musicals, without the least pretension. Every time I saw him he seemed genuinely enthused about something. He didn't have to drink to prove his manhood, or bully anyone, or hide behind an angry façade. In short, he was just himself, a happy person who appreciated the simple things of life, willing to share his enthusiasm with anyone who was interested.

Hal had a part-time job on Friday nights doing custodial work at a local church. On two or three occasions he invited me along.

I helped as best I could. To my amazement, he patiently taught me how to handle a heavy polishing machine, with its wide, spinning brush, and then trusted me to wax the floors. That trust was the first boost of self-esteem that I remember. I was contributing something of value — something I never experienced before.

In those few short hours he also taught me the joy of work.

I previously considered work as something tedious, a

curtailment of freedom necessary to live, but more like punishment than a blessing.

In stark contrast to this image was Hal — dramatically singing theatrical songs while cleaning the church hall — and that after completing a hard day's work.

He was obviously enjoying himself. No complaints. No rush to get things done. As different as dusting and polishing floors could be from teaching art, he was completely and joyously focused on what he was doing.

This presented an entirely different picture from the slavery I imagined. I absorbed his enthusiasm like a sponge. To this day, while working in the yard, I find myself singing tunes from *Man of La Mancha*.

Here was a man who could talk seriously one moment and then joke the next. He was strong yet never arrogant, despite his obvious talents. No posturing. No false bravado. Nothing phony about him at all. He even laughed at himself at times. And thoughtful? Despite working two jobs to support his family, he graciously swept the visiting boy next door into his world of *Fiddler on the Roof* and *Sound of Music*.

The humility he exhibited was never weak, self-effacing or insecure. Quite the opposite. It was open, alive and real. It carried him into the focus of every moment so he could experience it fully. Without trying, he showed me that humility is not something small or unmanly. It is the core of each man's being that comes alive when ego is set aside.

Hal never understood the important role he played in my life. Years later, when I looked him up and thanked him, he seemed perplexed. "What did I do?" he asked, somewhat confused and embarrassed.

I poorly explained how his example opened my eyes to new possibilities. I was in his debt for teaching me that I did not have to fit any *commercialized* image of manhood. None of us do. Authenticity comes from within, from expressing who we really are.

***

A year or two later, another person changed the direction of my life. His name was Joe, a neighbor of mine in Hartford, who had recently returned from military duty abroad. Even though we were neighbors, we had never so much as spoken before. At 12 years of age, I was more than 10 years younger than him.

One summer evening, I looked out the window of our third floor apartment. Joe was performing strange, deliberate movements in his backyard, almost like a robot. The motions seemed purposeful, almost combative, obviously following a prescribed set of rules.

Asian martial arts were not common in the U.S. back then, but I gradually understood that he was doing "something like karate." It was *tae kwon do*, a Korean martial art. The set of movements he practiced was called a *hyung* in Korean, or *kata* in Japanese.

Joe had studied tae kwon do from one of its most renown practitioners, a true master named Jhoon Rhee. While stationed in Japan, he also studied aikido, and developed a strong interest in the mystical side of the martial arts.

I remember watching his sharp, disciplined moves. They seemed an answer to my prayers.

I asked him to teach me. Having no interest, he politely refused. Over a period of days I quietly watched him from the other side of the fence that separated our backyards, no doubt looking like a wounded puppy. He finally agreed to take me on as a student.

He taught me at an agonizingly slow pace. The first lesson focused on how to situate my legs and posture into what was called a *front stance*. He then demonstrated how to walk while utilizing this stance, forward, backwards, and turning to the side. I learned nothing else for the first month while he practiced his exotic forms with brilliant speed and precision. Perhaps he did this to test my sincerity, or to discourage me from bothering him. Whatever his reason, his disinterested pace of teaching did not discourage me in the least. I practiced with unquestioned diligence, convinced that the rote motions would eventually lead to something my heart cried out for.

Joe eventually taught me the basic punches and kicks that characterized tae kwon do. We performed two-man practices where one person attacked while the other defended.

Proper form was everything to him. His focus on detail was contagious. He eventually taught me my first *hyung*.

I was hooked like never before. I was learning something ancient and mysterious, something that symbolized to me the transformation of a boy into manhood. I was fortunate to have someone like Joe to introduce me to this art. He opened up a whole new world of confidence and possibilities.

Back then, in the early '60s, martial arts were not commercialized as they are now. They were based on traditions that required an almost familial relationship between student and teacher. That I should be initiated into something so secretive and powerful made me feel like the luckiest kid on earth.

Joe exemplified everything that was special in the martial arts. He was patient, soft-spoken, polite and fearless. He spoke about philosophy and told me stories of strange feats performed by masters. The only part I failed to appreciate was meditating by the bushes at twilight when mosquitoes came out. Although he meditated alongside me with closed eyes, he still commented every time I twitched.

I lost touch with Joe soon after. Our paths intersected a few years later, just long enough to workout and take some photos in the backyard. Little did either of us know that my obsession with the martial arts would continue for decades to come. Immersing myself in the intricacies of different styles, I acquainted myself with the nuances of the warrior spirit. When it was my turn to eventually teach, I did my best to convey the philosophical patience that I learned from my reluctant neighbor.

***

Hal and Joe were very different from one another. Like two different worlds. Nevertheless, they had certain things in common: both were unobtrusive, self-made individuals of talent and personal discipline. Strong, passionate in their beliefs, yet inoffensive. As men, they cared enough to share their unique perspectives with an unrelated boy who needed them as mentors and role models.

Hal and Joe taught me that being a man is not the result of happenstance. It comes from self-discovery, self-development and a firm grasp of manly virtues — call them chivalry or not. There is a personal depth that must be tapped in order for the fullness of individuality to be real. This depth cannot be plumbed without the clear insight of humility.

Update: Decades after my experiences with Hal, I attended a church performance of *Camelot* which he directed.

The play moved me with its tragic undercurrents. Based on Thomas Mallory's *Le Morte d'Arthur*, it mourned the passing of chivalry's code of honor. This was my first introduction to King Arthur, Camelot, and the knights who exemplified this code. It sparked a long-standing passion for Arthurian literature.

Almost two decades later, it led to the writing of this book.

***

To appreciate the nuances of humility, it helps to understand the difference between *human-pride* and *ego-pride*. One serves as a true dynamic of life; the other does not.

Human-pride reflects the inner satisfaction that comes from doing the right thing without consideration of guilt, reward or punishment. It has nothing to do with feeling superior to someone else, as ego is wont to do. It is the simple fulfillment of human nature when we do what is right: working hard and well, caring for one's family and friends, learning a craft, mastering a challenge, defending a good cause without need for recognition. Human-pride is the contentment that comes from being true to who we are.

Human-pride is and always has been an unobtrusive source of creativity, tenacity, and self-esteem. It encourages us to respond to reality as is, and not just to how it relates to our ambitions. We feel its calm satisfaction when we obey laws that are just, and change those that are not. When it sparks our interest for a good cause, it becomes the source of tremendous energy and courage.

It does not come from the building or sustaining of a false image of oneself, or the desire to outshine someone else. It brings people together rather than keep them separate.

Ego-pride is very different. It is the anxiety that prompts us to create, sustain, or modify the image of ourselves that *we think* we project to others.

The Sanskrit word for ego, *ahamkara*, reveals some powerful insight. While the word *ego* is Latin for the pronoun *"I,"* ahamkara means *"I maker."* It describes ego as the impetus that constructs a false self-image. Through this image the ego then dominates the self in order to give it a semblance of "life." By translating everything according to the needs of this image, it impedes the directness of authenticity.

Ego-pride tries to convince us that we are *commodities* meant to compete with other commodities (other human beings). Our looks, talents, behaviors, intellect, popularity, even our sexuality can be subjugated by ego's will in its attempt to assert itself as something actually alive. It demands that we sacrifice our autonomy in order to enhance its marketability.

Ego-pride, in its obsession to be real, sees itself as the focal point of the universe.

Human pride, in contrast, lives as a center of the universe that has no circumference. We are all focal points of awareness.

While ego-pride is the antithesis of humility, human-pride generates its heart and soul.

***

Humility tells us that the first challenge to a knight-in-training is to defeat the metaphorical dragon that lives inside him — *his ego*. Only then can a proper hero be born.

Having encountered his dragon, today's image of a knight-errant is starting to take shape.

Humility prevents him from assuming that he has all the answers. He weighs evidence even against his own prejudices. With a clear mind, he uses the skills and talents he has developed to side with truth.

Most impressively, he is not a fool. His humility does not lend itself to the game of one-upmanship, gotcha politics or the tiresome antics of spin control. Because honesty is his measure, he has nothing fake that needs defending. His simplicity and directness outshines the blind assertiveness of extremism. The knight-errant is prepared for life's challenges. He knows that whether he wins or loses, he has already succeeded in the primary battle, which is choosing the right direction for his life.

As we examine the remaining principles of the Twelve Trusts of Chivalry-Now, we shall see how they contribute to building a complete man.

***

"It is enough that I know inside that what I do is the right thing."

This quote encapsulates the spirit of humility along with our entire chivalric code. It was written by a 15 year old from Florida who responded to one of our Chivalry-Now surveys.

Such words are not the resurrection of an antiquated, medieval code of honor. They reflect the activation of conscience on a personal and exciting level.

The seeds of chivalry are already implanted at every child's birth. The quest calls for us to nurture those seeds in ourselves as well as others so that virtue might someday flourish in the world.

Chapter 7

"Speak the Truth..."

Trust # 4: I will speak the truth at all times, and forever keep my word.

To facilitate our quest it helps to differentiate between two varia-tions of the word *truth.*

The first is the simplest. *Honesty.* Being a man of honor means speaking the truth at all times. Honorable men are dependable because their word is inviolate, a fundamental characteristic of the knight-errant.

But there is another side to truth that is more subtle yet far more grand. It refers to the underlying foundation of reality, something that exists whether we recognize it or not. While we might consider this foundation the ultimate mystery, it is found everywhere in everything we see, when we allow ourselves to see it.

Physical existence and nature are extensions of this *Truth,* and that includes us as well.

The spiritual aspect of Chivalry-Now recognizes that we are part of Truth, and that we have responsibilities toward it. We will come back to this later.

The first concept, speaking the truth at all times, is not always easy to follow. Expressing truth sometimes conflicts with the expectations of others. In a world where illusions and half-truths and following the crowd are values that many hold dear, hearing a contrary opinion, no matter how true, is not always welcome. It can challenge the status quo, disturb long-held patterns of belief, and make you unwelcome. It can actually separate you from those who insist on uniformity of beliefs, be they friends, family, or business associates.

There are groups that expect you to think a certain way, to vote for a particular candidate, and advocate for a particular agenda. They want to control who you are, and will use party loyalty or even references to God to acquire that power and exercise that control. Their hold can be so strong that even drastic error is ignored for the sake of a particular ideology, with terrible consequences.

The result of their efforts is a democracy that has lost its way, stifling free will and intelligence, and replacing them with what amounts to a *cult* mentality.

The need for mindless followers demonstrates how fearful such people are. They discourage free thought in order to garner support. They preach liberal or conservative takeovers, heaven and hell, Armageddon, unisex restrooms... anything to manipulate people's opinions.

Chivalry-Now rejects this for what it is, an enemy of freedom and democracy, and an insult to us all. In order for democracy to work we need the wisdom of well-informed, free thinking people who truly want the best for their country and for the world. Anything less is an affront to all that is best in humanity.

***

Honesty comes from confidently saying that what you think is true. The validity of your word, your honor as a man, depends on this. Just because someone told you something is true, or you read it in a book, no matter how authoritative or well intentioned, does not mean it is true. It is up to you to exercise your power of reason to determine that. That means being open to all sides of the issues, and thinking clearly and carefully, without prejudice.

This takes an inquisitive mind of strong integrity. It requires intelligence. That is why self-development, educating ourselves in mind and spirit, is the first principle of the Twelve Trusts. Without it, our capabilities are limited.

***

One of the many blessings of chivalry is the depth of meaning it adds to our perspective. We find deeper meaning even in something as simple as the concept of honesty.

On the surface, honesty means speaking the truth, and not pretending to be what one is not. As human beings, we have the capacity of speaking honestly one moment, and falsely the next. Chivalry compels us to choose the former.

It is possible for a man to be honest, but not chivalrous. That's because chivalry incorporates other values as well. A man may be honest in a needlessly hurtful or destructive way. He may gossip and delight in scandal. This is hardly compassionate, or manly behavior. It is projecting an empty image of superiority by pointing to someone else's fall. It lacks humility, justice and respect for humanity.

By infusing one's character with the full gamut of male virtues, chivalry injects still another necessary component: *sincerity*.

The authentic man carries a sincere commitment to truth that reflects itself in everything he does. Because this originates in his soul, it is not just imitative behavior, it is the man himself, his character. He becomes a man of truth, rather than someone using truth for momentary gain.

***

Drawing from principles we have examined so far, the image of our new knight-errant continues to shape itself. He is a humble man of deep character who develops his life for the greater good. Honesty and sincerity come naturally to him, constituting a moral base that enhances the other chivalric principles.

Our inclusion of *sincerity* finds vital support from many great men of the past:

– *John Tillotson*, Archbishop of Canterbury, 1630-1694.
"Sincerity is to speak as we think, to do as we pretend and profess, to perform what we promise, and really to be what we would seem and appear to be."

– *Socrates*, Greek philosopher, 469-399 B.C.E.
"The shortest and surest way to live with honor in the world is to be in all reality what we would appear to be; all human virtues increase and strengthen themselves by the practice and experience of them."

– *Samuel Taylor Coleridge*, English poet, 1772-1834.
"The whole faculties of man must be exerted in order to call forth noble energies; and he who is not earnestly sincere lives in but half his being, self-mutilated, self paralyzed."

– *William Shakespeare*, English poet, playwright and dramatist, 1564-1616.
"His words are his bonds, his oaths are oracles; his love sincere, his thoughts immaculate; his tears, pure messengers sent from his heart; his heart as far from fraud, as heaven from earth."

– *Confucius*, Chinese moral teacher.
"Sincerity and truth are the basis of every virtue."

***

Telling the truth is sometimes painful.

Some time ago, I found myself in a strange predicament. I was in a position where telling the truth would allow someone else's vicious lies to be directed against me. A simple denial on my part would have nullified the entire situation.

I chose to tell the truth, even though I knew it would harm my entire future, and benefit the person who lied.

Despite everything, I never regretted telling the truth. I knew I was living the principles I believed in, and I bore the consequences that followed knowing that they were unjust.

Those who knew me understood what was happening and were very supportive. In their eyes, I had defined myself as an honest man more than any amount of writing about chivalry could.

The person who lied smugly walked away with a marred reputation that continues to this day. No real friends. No relationships based on trust. No understanding of what was lost.

Perhaps they do not care, but people who believe that it is okay to lie, or feel they can profit by doing so, have no idea what they do to themselves. Falsehood detracts from their very being and cannot be easily remedied. In effect, they live what they profess: a lie.

What are we if not advocates for truth? If we embrace lies for personal gain, or to harm someone else, the falsehood we profess ends up shaping who we are. False men. False people. False pride. Never happy or genuinely welcomed or accepted. Never loved.

Integrity and honor are not things that we can claim for the asking. They are qualities that we earn or never have. They reflect who we are through our actions and beliefs. Truth provides the core of this dynamic. Lies and pretense transform the incredible possibilities of human potential into abominations.

***

Four major opponents to honesty need to be confronted.

The first is the kind of *laziness* that comes from confusion and indoctrination. It takes effort to discover what is true and then stand up for it. The lazy mind does not bother.

The second opponent is that of *fear*. We run a certain risk by disagreeing with accepted opinions. We risk being ostracized from family or friends who disagree with us. In Western democracies, freedom of speech is guaranteed, but the reaction to that speech from others is not. Nevertheless, we cannot let popular disagreement hamper our honest expression of what we believe.

The third has to do with the tacit acceptance that *it is okay to be dishonest* in the name of power or profit. We see this in various degrees everywhere we look, from subtly false advertising to blatant political lies. Here we find the slippery slope that contributes to the lack of outrage we suffer from today. We have learned to accept a measure of dishonesty with a complacent shrug. *"What did you expect? It's business. It's politics. All's fair in love and war."*

The fourth is *prejudice*. Like it or not, we all carry prejudices. One of the challenges in our search for truth involves struggling against preconceived ideas in order to see beyond them. The struggle can be intense at times, but it becomes easier as we develop a thirst for liberation.

Once we recognize these four opponents, really recognize them for what they are, we cross the threshold of a new awakening. We find the integrity we need to look for truth in everything, and this contributes to developing a noble character.

Expanding knowledge is a worthy endeavor, not just for ourselves but for everyone. We may have to contend with those who resent new thinking, or feel threatened by new ideas, but the task is vital to who we are in relationship to the quest — which is our life.

***

Spiritual *Truth* opens the door to the full dimension of our quest.

Male ethics cannot be complete without attending to the entire man: moral, physical, intellectual and *spiritual*. By spiritual I do not mean in a religious sense, which would exclude non-believers. It is important to our cause to be as inclusive as possible. All men of sincerity are welcome.

To facilitate discussion, I use words like *spirit, spirituality* and *soul* to refer to that aspect of human nature in which the sum of our being is greater than its parts.

Human beings are a unique composite of consciousness, instinct, cognition, reason and emotions. The combination of these attributes results in a self-awareness that surpasses the individual attributes themselves. While self-awareness is merely a by-product of the physical brain, it produces something almost magical: the conscious wonderment that underlies self-reflection and our confrontation with the world.

This awareness is *us*, in the depth of our being and the height of our aspirations. To call it *soul* detracts nothing from the perspective of those who are religious, or those who are not. For our purposes, spirituality refers to the incredibly complex expression of life that we are part of and experience first-hand. Here we find our greatest value and potential —everything that we are, which includes the possibility of becoming more.

***

When you think of it, our consciousness of the world borders on nothing less than what seems miraculous.

We are not the largest, strongest or quickest creatures in the world. We do not live the longest. Our errors are many and sometimes catastrophic. Despite all that, the complexity of our brains, our minds if you will, makes us the most advanced, complicated and influential creatures in the universe. (As far as we know at this time.)

Our conscious decisions impact the world and everything in it — for good or ill. Our beliefs, our relationships, the causes we support, the issues we ignore, the waste we generate, technology, our vision of the future — all these things and more effect the world around us. We cannot afford haphazard choices, a lack of concern, loyalty to misguided agendas, environmental ruin, or neglect of our neighbors' well being. Thanks to technology and a globalized population, the kind of greed that we once got away with is no longer acceptable, and could lead to our extinction. A lot of powerful people know this, but just do not care.

There is a greater Truth that we are part of. Undefined. Inter-related. All-inclusive. Not some metaphysical phenomenon that we need to unite with or bow down to. Just the common sense inclusiveness that we see when metaphysical jargon is put aside.

The framework is simple. For *ultimate* Truth to be ultimate, by definition, it must include everything. The inter-dependency we see at all levels reveals a fragile yet tenacious complexity. The environment we depend on includes clean air, clean water, and healthy forests and wildlife to maintain its life-sustaining balance, which J.E. Lovelock referred to as *Gaia* (see *Gaia, A New Look at Life on Earth*). This dependency could easily be disrupted by greedy people who disregard the obvious, or have no regard for the continuation of our species beyond personal gain. Our present standards are so low that we consider many of these people upstanding citizens.

It is plain to see that we are part of the universe around us. As creatures capable of thought and reason, however, we are responsible to the universe for the choices that we make.

Another word for Truth in this context is *Mystery*. Here we recognize our basic ignorance of the world we live in, the life that sustains us and, most boggling of all, existence itself. There are fundamental questions about the universe and about our-selves that we just cannot explain. The fact that we have no explanations does not deny that existence is real, or that the spark of life that informs us is more than our present scope of biology can explain.

No matter what we believe or fail to believe, Mystery is there, silent, transparent, ever-present. Everything we see, including us, would not exist except for the paradox of something coming from nothing. It is this incomprehensible magician's hat where our train of reason crashes — yet we must accept it. Here we find the question mark that affirms the validity of our inquiry, even as the answers evade us.

Mystery and Truth represent grand concepts that we recognize but don't understand. We need to include these concepts in order to relate with the universe as comprehensively as possible. We exist; we see the world around us; we see our dependency on nature, along with the inter-dependency of all life. Bit-by-bit we expand our knowledge base, challenging ourselves to explore what we do not yet understand.

This is basic to scientific inquiry — and to moral inquiry as well.

That things exist, instead of a profound *Nothing*, is inexplicable at this time. We have yet to imagine what preceded the Big Bang. The logic of cause and effect tells us that the universe should not exist at all — and yet it does. Our lack of understanding does not negate what is or what happened in the past, or the importance of what we do not yet know. By referring to this as Mystery, we acknowledge that which we do not yet know as part of the equation, like an algebraic symbol yet to be defined. We include and can therefore ponder the indefinable.

By acknowledging what we do not know, without prejudice, along with what we do know, our minds open up to a more expansive vision that transcends our limitations. This reflects the kind of humility discussed earlier, and validates its importance. Humility defines our relationship with the universe with the moral integrity that our principles demand. We are honor-bound to protect the world we live in.

***

How does one approach or relate to this grand, mysterious Truth?

I can think of only one answer: *In reverential awe.*

By recognizing that our conscious minds are part of Truth we are invited, by what we call the *quest,* to decipher its mysteries. The quest is nothing more than purposely confronting life as an adventure from which we learn and grow. It is a search for meaning, self-discovery and personal development. In simple terms, it is a commitment to finding what was lost.

I include some presumptions that might cause scientists to instinctively balk, such as suggesting that human beings have special purpose or meaning in a world built by the random impartiality of evolution.

My words suggest a planner or inherent purpose that the theory of evolution refuses to postulate. As the vanguards of knowledge, scientists have every right to challenge this. What I point out to them is that a large group of planners who were not here at the beginning have since arrived, workers who *purposely* change their environment, philosophers able to decipher and articulate meaning.

I am talking about *us.* We are all conscious children of evolution.

Our ability to think and reason and define value has thus been added to forces of the universe. The world of today is not as it was four billion years ago. Our arrival makes the Earth a different planet than it was.

The impact of our presence is either good or bad, depending on our choices.

When we relegate human evolution to haphazard chance, or allow it to be directed by greed and a thirst for power (as we are doing now), we get less than admirable results. If we implement a wiser, moral, even cooperative approach, we produce something very different.

We do not have to surrender to our worst instincts. We have powers of reason. We have intelligence. We have science. We have compassion, justice, mercy... and above all, Truth. In other words, we can choose to take a responsible, proactive stance for the good of our planet, and all the creatures on it.

***

We find veiled reference to such ideas in the legends of King Arthur.

Heaped with Christian symbolism while harkening back to pagan times, stories of the *Grail* provide road signs pointing to the inexplicable. Here we find mythical symbols and archetypal clues that are imbedded in our psyche, a wealth of knowledge long hoarded in our collective sub-conscious. They provide a treasure-trove of insights gleaned from centuries of confronting Mystery itself.

The Grail stories concern themselves with a mysterious object of veneration called the Grail. This object is usually described as a chalice or cup, but sometimes as a jewel or stone, platter or basin. Christian legends identify it as the cup Jesus used at the Last Supper. A recent theory, popularized by books like the *Da Vinci Code*, suggests that the Grail was actually a person, Mary Magdalene, who carried the bloodline of Jesus into Europe. These theories do not explain the more ancient and universal symbolism that the Grail provides as its spiritual heritage.

The protagonist of the more popular renditions is a young, inexperienced knight named Sir Perceval. While visiting a mysterious castle, he sees a brilliantly shining cup paraded through the Great Hall and venerated by the inhabitants. Perceval restrains himself from asking what it is.

Like many of us, when Mystery first presents itself, he failed to respond. This lack of inquiry is significant not only to Perceval's quest, but to our own. Unlike most mythical journeys, Perceval is not challenged by a threat, or required to answer a riddle. *He is expected to ask the proper questions.* Because he does not, the Grail and its mysterious castle vanish from sight.

When we fail to question things, we confront the mystery of the universe with indifference or the audacity of a closed mind. The opportunity passes. Truth vanishes into the background.

The guardian of this relic, the Fisher King, suffers from a painful wound that will not heal. Years earlier, while jousting, the splinter from a broken lance pierced his testes and remained there. This symbol of wounded manhood is just as valid today as it was a thousand years ago — perhaps more so. Giving ourselves to the trappings of belligerence and competitiveness, we have lost the depth of who we really are.

One of the tragedies of the Fisher King's wound is that his pain is reflected on the world around him. His realm becomes an impoverished *Wasteland*, which lays low the people who live there.

The symbolism is obvious. When men lose sight of who they are as men, the whole world suffers.

According to the story, all this would have been rectified if Perceval had asked the right questions.

We are experiencing the same situation now. Manhood has been wounded by the loss of male ethics, resulting in a faltering, broken culture and constant war, pushing everything off balance. We have created a world of violence and deception, abuse and greed. Crimes against the environment appear to be leading us to the proverbial Wasteland.

When Perceval learns what was expected of him, he is filled with remorse. Typical of the chivalrous heart, he seeks to find the Grail Castle again to set things right.

In similar fashion, here we are, living in an unexplained universe, grounded in Mystery, watching the world we live in being ravaged by war, poverty and pollution. What causes us to ignore these major problems, and to fixate, instead, on the score of the latest ball game, or the pitifully desperate lives of celebrities, or how to get rich?

We fail the test, not through ignorance, like Perceval, but because our culture failed to teach us how to think more profoundly. Since the waning of the Age of Enlightenment, we have become small, un-heroic people, obsessed by triviality, gossip and personal greed. We are like the Fisher King, wounded in the masculine qualities of our souls by complacency and a lack of definition, assuming with little concern that someone else will set things right.

We are like Perceval as well. We did not create this situation, but the purity we find in our hearts, if only we look there, can and will remedy it.

With toxic waste sites, contaminated water supplies and the dangers of global warming, the dire threat of an impending Wasteland calls for immediate action. We are willfully destroying our planet, suffering all the while yet failing to ask why.

After many adventures, Sir Perceval finds his way to the Grail Castle. This time, when the Grail is paraded through the hall, he asks the right questions:

What is the secret of the Grail? Whom does it serve?

With that simple act, the Fisher King is healed, the land recovers, and young Perceval takes his place as heir apparent.

The questions we need to ask are similar: *What is the Mystery we are part of? How do we serve it best?*

The spiritual side of Chivalry-Now points out that there is more to life than combating evil and confronting dragons. There is a Mystery that follows us everywhere we go. We see hints of it in glorious sunsets, or while pondering the infinity of stars, or appreciating the intricate detail of a dragonfly's wing. Wordless. Selfless. Almost time-stopping. Transcendent of thought or explanation. The experience carries an affirmation of certitude.

It has been said that this *mystical experience* is not unusual, but occurs to us all at some point in our lives. I do not know if that is true. It is my hope that each of us, like Perceval, receives an eye-opening splash of Mystery now and then as a personal invitation to set things right. What happens next depends on us.

It happened to me in my mid-twenties, and my whole perspective of life changed by the edge of a lake at sunset. I recognized that I was part of that Mystery, and I wanted to learn more. From that moment on, I have searched to find the hidden meaning behind everything I see, hoping to be part of that never-ending quest to set things right.

It would be a mistake to conclude, however, that I am nothing more than a "mystically inclined" dreamer. I am not moved by esoteric explanations, hidden gospels, or the application of myth beyond archetypal relevance. What does move me is the direct experience of life itself, without misleading explanations. I want knowledge that increases my experience of life, that enhances my vision of the world, and helps me make better decisions. I am wary of the proverbial *leap of faith* that calls me to place judgment aside for the bliss of baseless certainty. But this is *my* life. *Mine.* I want to know what is true and what is not.

Is it the same for you?

Our confrontation with Truth, with Mystery, does not come with a guidebook or directions. Some may enjoy its momentary thrill as they might appreciate the experience of beauty. Others consider it no more than a passing sensation. A few might reject it as a threat to everything they believe. Those who are religiously inclined might translate it into theological terms, and respond as they will from there.

What really matters to us, however, is how *we* respond.

Chivalry-Now, like its medieval predecessor, urges us to respond with our whole being. When we perceive Mystery, when we relate it to everything we see and do, we become more complete human beings in relationship to Truth. We treat people better. We respect and love the world we live in.

The Grail experience affirms the central meaning of the Genesis story, that the world is good. Here we find spiritual validation for the principles of Chivalry-Now. By responding to the Grail inside us, we stride forward to learn deeper truths every day of our lives. In this way we connect the transitory nature of our lives to the continuum we are part of. Here we find subtle meanings that normally escape us, answers that we each have to find for ourselves. Without that connection to Mystery, we remain incomplete. Our spiritual drive is thwarted.

Chivalry-Now calls us as individuals to relate with Truth on all levels in an honest and forthcoming way. Not as passive followers, but as active seekers. It calls us to think and feel with full consciousness of the moment, seeing beyond illusions that otherwise deceive us.

Chapter 8

"Defend Those in Need…"

Trust # 5: I will defend those who cannot defend themselves.

There was a boy who lived in my old neighborhood in Hartford. His name was Nelo, a strapping young lad, born of Italian immigrants. He was not a regular among our small circle of neighbors, but he appeared now and then for whatever reason. Although we didn't know him well, everyone respected him.

Our respect was intuitive. Despite his being older and stronger, he treated everyone fairly and never acted like a bully. No gossip. No bickering. He owed none of us anything, yet he always seemed ready to stand up for what was right. In short, he was the stuff that boy-heroes are made from.

One day, he saw a teenager twice my size push me into the bushes for no apparent reason. Nelo immediately interceded, protecting me from further abuse. That would have been enough to warrant my youthful adulation, but it did not end there. He later taught me some boxing moves so I could defend myself in the future, laying the groundwork for what later became a strong interest in the martial arts.

Keep in mind, we were never really friends or close in any way. Nelo did not see me as a friend, but as someone who needed help. He would have done the same for anyone. He was a prime example of instinctive male chivalry — protecting others while asking nothing in return.

I would describe his character as noble, despite his humble origins in the south end of Hartford. He had the kind of nobility of the soul that strong, manly character is made of.

I think most of us have encountered people like Nelo. The

world is a better place because of them. The legacy of the knight-errant manages to survive in the hearts of such men.

***

For every young hero like Nelo, there are scores of people who reject helping others. Their justification? "It's not my problem."

This attitude is the antithesis of chivalry and manhood.

Injustice is everyone's concern — not just morally, but practically as well. Apathy poisons any culture, especially when we lack a sufficient number of strong willed people to counteract it. (This is as much a moral imperative for women as men, but the focus of this book is on male ethics; women speak well for themselves.)

History shows that good things happen when people fight for what is right. With each success, hope is encouraged, ideals are strengthened and humanity itself is elevated. The whole world benefits.

When we buy into the debilitating vision that says "it's not my problem," we reject what is best and sacred in us all.

Remember that Cain, the person in the Bible who made a similar statement when he asked "Am I my brother's keeper?" was guilty of killing his own brother.

This does not mean we have to leap up to fight for every cause. There are too many causes and too little time. We start by caring for the well-being of those who are closest, and widen that circle every day. We choose our battles and support those issues that are closest to our heart, including global issues. Eventually we learn that the whole world is our family.

Discernment is important when choosing a worthy cause. We should evaluate its merit, feasibility and ultimate goals, and keep an open mind even after we commit ourselves. Worthy causes, like people, can change unpredictably. They get political and sometimes unreasonable in their demands. Do not hesitate to make changes or walk away if circumstances warrant. A chivalrous mind does not run on automatic pilot. It makes informed choices by weighing the facts carefully.

When people close their minds to the ramifications of their acts or beliefs, consequences can be horrible. Mob lynchings. Ethnic cleansing. Religious wars. Inquisitions. Barring children from classrooms because of skin color or ethnicity. Such atrocities occur when we fail to question the ongoing morality of our own beliefs.

***

We often do fail to question our actions and beliefs.

We say we believe in equal rights even as we continue discriminatory practices.

We believe in fair play, yet use every trick in the book in order to win.

Some of us fall in love with women and then abuse them without an ounce of conscience.

We say our democratic nation is ruled by the will of the people. How is it that, when people protest against what they consider an unjust war they are labeled unpatriotic, told that they are undercutting the troops (that the war puts in harm's way), and even accused of assisting the enemy? Such name-calling is little more than political propaganda and emotional blackmail.

There are religions claiming to be based on the Gospel that blatantly contradict the words of Jesus, and no one questions them. Jesus told people to pray in private, yet school prayer has become a national issue. When he said *blessed are the poor,* it has somehow been translated as favoring the rich. *Love thy neighbor as thyself,* has been twisted to mean loving only those who support a particular political agenda. Certain preachers insist that we turn a blind eye to the health of the environment, despite references that we should be stewards of the earth.

We sometimes have to defend people from the hypocrisy of our own popular errors — political, secular and religious. We have to clarify what we believe in, not by accepting the beliefs of others, but by thinking things through on our own. Only then can we identify hypocrisy for what it is.

We become real men, assured in our essence and unafraid, when we embrace the ethics that define us as such. The CEO in his ivory tower, the politician who basks in his popularity, the preacher who plays to your weaknesses to make you feel good, the aberrant rock singer or movie star — they miss the point entirely if they do not step forward and defend the integrity of our world. What good is their money and popularity if they serve only themselves?

***

By acting strong, compassionate and honorable in everything we do, we best fulfill our obligations to the world we live in, and to ourselves. This is why chivalry tells us to be *men* first in everything we do.

Defending those in need is part of a time-honored code of manly tradition recognized by all cultures. Doing so gives purpose to our strength and daring beyond the limits of selfish concerns. This is one of the ways that society morally benefits from chivalric principles.

Unfortunately, our commercialized world teaches a very different message. We are told in a thousand demeaning ways that our sole obligation is to adopt a self-centered, *consumer* mentality. We are encouraged to be vain, to hoard wealth, to take and take, and give little in return. I have met men who love their cars more than their wives. And while there were always dregs of healthy men who preferred living off a woman's labor or welfare check rather than carry their own weight, today they have the audacity to brag about it. In this topsy-turvy culture, where male ethics are all but forgotten, they actually think they are clever, *even manly*, by shirking their basic responsibilities.

For far too long we have allowed male values to be degraded by those who profit by doing so. Exploiters would rob us of everything that is human if it meant an increase in sales. They portray our sisters as sexual objects, and feed young minds with crass images of sensuality that undercut any realistic concept of love. They use every means they can get away with to manipulate minds to their way of thinking. They want us to forget the independence that manhood implies because a sharp, thoughtful mind is not easily controlled. To a large extent, they have succeeded. Without a viable cultural ethic resisting every inch of the way, their commercialization of the world has so overwhelmed us that we can scarcely imagine anything different.

They have created a world with little room for conscience. We are taught to turn a blind eye as they attack the humanity of our wives and sisters and children, and us as well. We surrender to this vision of incessant greed at the cost of what is real and valuable. We have traded our freedom for a marketplace homogeneity of pleasure over responsibility, distraction over the attentiveness of living, and the surest sign of breakdown, the idolization of so-called celebrities who contribute nothing to the betterment of the world.

What made all this possible was the loss of a viable male ethic to counteract it. The resulting void in our culture has been filled by an inadequate philosophical dynamic already in place. Capitalism. The marketplace now holds powerful control over our national, political, cultural and moral ethics. Even religion shapes itself more and more according to supply-side economics. Capitalism definitely has its place, but needs to be reconnected to its original intent and domain. Economics do not define right from wrong, or generate love of neighbor, or adhere to the

Golden Rule, or teach boys how to become men. That is the responsibility of family and culture. Unfortunately, due to gaps in our cultural mores, capitalism has replaced the Golden Rule with a poor substitute: what symbolically can be described as a Golden Calf.

To counter this, it is more important than ever to defend those in need, because those in need include us all.

***

"No greater love is this, than a man give up his life for another."

The propensity toward sacrifice in women is obvious and vital to our species. This includes the personal inconvenience of pregnancy, labor pains associated with birth, and the constant dedication to a child's growth and well-being. For the most part, women are the mainstay of family life, just as men were once considered the breadwinner.

Motherhood can almost be described as a loss of independent selfhood for the safeguard of someone else. *No greater love is this…* But it is wrong to think of their sacrifice as personal loss. It is usually a freely given gift motivated by love and maternal instinct. Nothing is more beautiful or contributes more to the survival of our species. Most mothers would lay down their lives to protect their children.

For men it is the same, yet somewhat different. The urge to protect and defend one's mate and progeny remain a strong part of the male psyche, as are other acts of self-sacrifice, less noticed than women's because they are indirect. Dedication to the workplace where labor is unseen by the family cannot compete with the intimacy of lullabies, and comforting a child who has scraped a knee. Their sacrifice is just as real and time-consuming, but goes into paying such things as rent, utilities, food and clothing, instead of constant, hands-on attention.

These quick summaries describe generalizations that have

changed over the last few decades. Workplaces are frequented as much by women as by men, producing indirect self-sacrifice of women by day on top of motherhood by night. To make matters worse, many women support single parent households, where the male presence and contribution is nearly or completely absent or, in the case of male parasites, actually contributes to the financial burden.

Of course there are many fathers who break the stereotypes as well. They contribute strong and attentive parenting skills, sharing equal responsibilities with their wives. I'm proud to have two nephews and a son-in-law who are excellent fathers and husbands. None of them would be considered unmanly. One of my nephews served as an EMT, the other as a forest firefighter.

Unfortunately, a portion of men end up adopting a tough guy image, purportedly masculine, that resists sacrificing anything for anyone.

At home, he lets his wife do all the work and parenting while he commits himself to the television. He shows no interest or enthusiasm for his children. He might do well by them financially out of a sense of pride, or waste his money on alcohol and entertainment.

If this stereotype were all inclusive, men certainly do not come off very well. We appear less compassionate than women, less attentive to our children, more selfish, more reluctant to give of ourselves or sacrifice anything. To the degree this is true, it is appropriate for men to be ashamed.

Thankfully, there is another side to male sacrifice that needs to be recognized. Without dismissing valiant female counterparts, men are traditionally the ones who work in emergency services, such as police or firefighters. They join the military by the millions, sacrificing a measure of their lives to preparing for the battlefield, where many sacrifice life and limb to protect their nation, family, way of life, and the comrades by their sides.

At times, even klutzy, awkward, inarticulate men perform

heroic feats of bravery. Some humbly refuse to take credit for their deeds.

Chivalry recognizes this sacrifice as a dedicated expression of love — somewhat different from those of motherhood, yet just as real. Less obvious than parenting, it is still related to the instinct of protecting kin, that widens to include others as well. Here we find motivation for our heroic impulses, even martyrdom, that so entices the male gender.

One does not volunteer for such hazards without strong inclinations of protectiveness, loyalty and duty. Placing one's life at risk contradicts the tendency to avoid danger for the sake of self-survival. And yet millions of men do this, men from every class, region and culture.

Reasons for joining the military are many. A fellow might be looking for challenge or adventure, or educational benefits, or want to see the world. He may be looking for a meaningful rite-of-passage — many men do. Perhaps his family has long military traditions he wants to continue, or the country needs him for defense, or to protect national borders, or respond to natural disasters.

No matter what reason, the attraction to self-sacrifice remains. Daily fatalities during war time remind us how serious military commitment is. Soldiers get hurt, maimed and killed — sometimes for causes they do not believe in. Their dedication speaks well for the depth of their souls.

***

What is a chivalrous knight if not a spiritual warrior dedicated to what is true and good? Warriors are born to resist enemies in order to protect those they cherish and the causes they believe in.

The chivalrous heart knows that there are things worth fighting for. There are pacifists who disagree, and I respect their views. I respect all opinions that are honest, well thought out and morally based. For men of chivalry, however, extreme pacifism is too limiting a commitment. It deprives the vitality of their *warrior spirit*.

The warrior spirit provides a particular mix of qualities that contribute to our overall humanity. Today's sensibilities might not recognize them at first, associating them with war and killing and brutality, but the warrior spirit transcends bellicosity. Exploring its rich depth, we discover:

- An intensity for life filled with the energy and readiness to act when needed.
- A desire to perfect oneself for the benefit of others.
- A determination to protect one's family, neighborhood, nation and world.
- Doing one's best in everything.
- Being true to oneself, and to others.
- Honesty. Loyalty. Integrity.
- Fairness and the willingness to stand up for what is right, even when everyone is against you.
- Idealism joined with reality.
- A sense of duty greater than one's own needs.

While these attributes contribute to the mindset of a good soldier, they are qualities of the soul that can benefit us all. We are less for the want of them. The warrior spirit is part of the ideal man, and therefore a vital part of chivalry. It has nothing to do with being *warlike*, or immoral, or violent by nature. No one dreads war as much as the soldier who must face it.

True warriors recognize that civilized men should be able to respectfully discuss conflicts and come to reasonable solutions. Nations should do the same. Cooperation and peaceful coexistence should be everyone's goal.

But men and nations do not always adhere to civilized requirements. Politicians are not soldiers and see war differently.

We do not live in a perfect world. Sometimes it is necessary to strongly defend the rights of the innocent, or the downtrodden or victims of aggression. Sometimes we have to put our lives at risk for worthy causes. One needs to be prepared for violence in order to resist it. Without this personal commitment, men are incomplete in the eyes of chivalry.

This is where strength of character outweighs strength of limb. All a man has to do is lift weights to build physical strength, or act rudely to appear aggressive. This says nothing about resolve, compassion for others or strength of character. Defending the innocent is a choice of will based on one's values, which is why it is listed in the Twelve Trusts.

***

Back in 2005, I was privileged to do some work for the U.S. Coast Guard's Research and Development Center. I was thoroughly impressed by the quality of purpose exhibited by the men and women in uniform who worked there. For the most part, they put their egos behind them, focused on their objectives, and displayed all the discipline and cooperation that Chivalry-Now could ever hope to propagate.

The Coast Guard is a military institution. Its purpose is to protect our country, not through military ventures around the world, but by responding to threats of terrorism, natural disaster, narcotics trade, and illegal immigration. It is the only government agency that responded to *Hurricane Katrina* flawlessly, and even then refused to take credit. Chivalry again. They accomplished their mission as they always do, rescuing people relentlessly until the job is done.

Here I found the warrior tradition at its finest: men and women who were highly trained, committed to their purpose, and working cooperatively for the greater good. Courtesy was a base dynamic at all times. Their indomitable spirit of the warrior had nothing to do with killing or war.

What do we have if we discard such energy and commitment, or rob them of their purpose? A safer world? Universal peace? A new Eden? Most likely a soulless passivity that scarcely merits the paradise it hopes to find.

The warrior spirit is consciously open to the world. It is a spirit of honor that does its best to avoid, compensate for, or defeat what is bad or hurtful. It intimately knows the benefits of sacrifice, and does its best to avoid scandal.

I believe the warrior spirit is in us all to a greater or lesser extent. It can be used to rid the world of sexism, racism, and the ethnocentricity that tries to impose its will on other nations. It can eliminate the contentious lack of civility that is now commonplace, while encouraging voices to speak up for what is right.

All of this is part of Chivalry-Now too.

***

The instinct to protect goes beyond particular vocations.

When times are dangerous, efforts are made to protect women and children first, as evidenced during the sinking of the Titanic. While this may be seen as a cultural tradition (stemming from chivalry), it is based on a deeper instinct, that of defending those in need, family especially. Our natural impulse is to protect those we love, and those with whom we identify.

When a man succeeds at that, he is recognized as a hero, which is every young boy's dream. When he fails, he is branded a coward, every boy's nightmare.

While our culture no longer focuses on self-sacrifice, and tends to honor vain, egocentric, power-hungry men, who are decidedly un-heroic, the heroic message still manages to filter out through popular culture and traditional means. Movies, comic books, television shows, computer games, sports — all convey heroic images that the male psyche responds to. While their moral overtones are usually superficial, the underlying message comes through loud and clear, connecting with something deeply embedded in our DNA.

Myth, legend and heroic tales provided this in the past, supplemented by participating in the hunt or combat training, where the spirit of the warrior could be tested in trial and deed. The seriousness of life was paramount to this experience, promoting honesty, sincerity, focus, and the development of personal character.

What we have today is little more than fantasy in comparison, conveying messages that stir the heart for an hour or two, and then set us adrift. We long for something more real, more significant than stock-trading, or the latest episode of some police drama, or rooting like a maniac for the touchdown of a favorite team. We long for something that is worthy, something that will test male courage.

It is in our power, here and now, to reclaim the heritage of our warrior spirit. We need only to look inside, awaken that spirit, and apply it to the way we live. The warrior spirit is not some mindless energy we only tap into while dancing around a bonfire. It is the perspective we get when we incorporate male principles into real life.

***

Rising to the defense of those who cannot defend themselves is a moral imperative for every man. More often than not, however, we ignore what happens around us. Our natural instinct for defending the weak has surrendered to the apathy of amoral economics. Compared to what lies dormant inside us, we have become sad, pathetic creatures, neglecting our deepest vision for the cheap thrill of distraction. We see the problems of the world, but have withheld our outrage for so long we can scarcely find it anymore. We close ourselves off, focus on hobbies or sports or the television clicker, where we still feel a sense of control — and in doing so, degenerate into something small, unheroic, spiritually bereft. In time, we disregard everything beyond the shrinking plastic-wrap of our own personal boundaries. We may complain about the system or politics, but only as half-converted victims who enjoy complaining — too impotent to make a difference.

There are reasons for this.

Early in life we think we can change the world. Our concept of right and wrong is simple. That changes as we grow up. Life's harsh complexities chip away at our idealism and innocence. Problems seem overwhelming at times — solutions all too costly or fleeting. We are told that it is better to avoid than confront. Don't make waves.

The fact that today's society does not encourage male qualities beyond the narrow competitiveness of the sports arena or board room contributes to the diminishment of our ideals. Our culture provides no mooring of genuine significance for men. Our initiative fades away.

It is difficult buying into a society that does not buy into you.

***

Those who exploit us do not want us to be free. They do not want us to think for ourselves, or challenge the way things are. As long as we remain small and petty, feeding our insecurities behind ridiculous outbursts of bravado, they continue to reap profits. They shape our values so that a million dollar salary seems reasonable for a talented baseball player, while hard-working men and women laboring in sweat shops can barely feed their families.

***

Every man wants to be a hero, and can be a hero to someone, or to a valuable cause.

There are many ways to be heroic, many causes that need champions. It may be your neighbor's son who needs a positive role model; or some woman being discriminated against on the job; or an elderly person longing for someone to talk with. Churches, synagogues and mosques can steer you toward worthy causes. You can volunteer for hospice, or at your local shelter or soup kitchen. Take an interest in shaping politics into something that works better for us. Join your volunteer fire department, or neighborhood watch. Inform yourself about the issues and make your opinion heard.

Wherever you go, whatever you do, always stand up for what is right. Be steadfast in your convictions, but politely open to correction.

There may be forces lined up against you. You might be the only one standing up for an unpopular cause, and will suffer rejection because of it. You may lose your job. Sometimes even thinking a little differently will ostracize you from the crowd.

Taking a stand always incurs risk, but isn't that what heroism is all about? Doing the right thing despite the cost?

There will be times when you let down your guard and occasionally slip. None of us are perfect. That is why we need an ethical code to remind us. The important thing is that we try, and keep on trying, no matter how many times we fail.

A code of ethics should not to be taken lightly, or referred to only when convenient. It is a life change. It purposely shapes you into a fine example of what it means to be a man.

In an ever-shrinking world that cries out for peace, under-standing and civility, what greater calling can there be?

Chapter 9

"Honor and Respect Women..."

Trust # 6: I will honor and respect women, and refute sexism in all its guises.

Chivalry-Now reflects the pedigree of its medieval sources by including a special recognition of women as one of its Twelve Trusts. This is broken down into two very different principles, each as important as the other: *respect for the person,* and *respect for the female gender as a whole.*

The first is simple and obvious. We are called to respect all people, no matter what gender, race or ethnicity. Martin Luther King explained it best when he told us to judge people according to the content of their character. That means respecting each person as a unique individual.

Prejudice is a strange, nonsensical phenomenon that contradicts common sense. In our relationships among men, we know first hand that no two men are alike. We easily take that as a given. That is obviously true of women as well. It is wrong to group people according to stereotypes. It steals away their individuality, and blocks our own recognition of truth. Every woman, like every man, has good points and bad, strengths and weaknesses, individual tastes and interests. They deserve to be recognized for such, and measured for who they are and not some dismissive stereotype.

This does not mean that generalized gender differences do not exist, and should not be recognized. A lot of individual diversity can be found in both sexes, with considerable overlap in each. The traditional boundary lines between gender roles have largely been erased. In the name of freedom and equality, that is a good thing despite certain cultural tremors. This breaking of confinement, however, does not eliminate gender differences. Dr. John Grey's popular series based on *Men are from Mars, Women are from Venus,* points out many of these differences, inferring that the different cultural perspectives of the genders make them seem like they are from different planets.

That we need to prove this today points to the hyper-sensitivity of political correctness in recent decades. Guilt for past transgressions, and ones that still persist, has resulted in intellectual hesitation. No one wants to be labeled a sexist or racist, and this has spawned a certain measure of fear and timidity. While this is understandable, fear and timidity are enemies of truth.

Not recognizing that gender differences exist may be the strangest prejudice of all.

Everywhere we look, the differences show themselves. At parties, men tend to drift into groups of other males, discussing their interests in their own particular ways. Women tend to drift into groups of females, and discuss very different topics. This is a generality, of course, but one we commonly see.

We also see shelves in bookstores loaded with books on women's issues, while books on male issues rarely outnumber a handful. Magazines cater to issues that are gender-based, and the results are quite astounding. For men, they are based mostly on sports and sex. For women, they include a wide range of everyday interests, fashion and repetitive advice. While one can argue that these tendencies reflect a certain amount of sexism, their popularity is telling. Differences do exist.

At one time, traditional career paths between men and women were more defined and restricted than they are today. Despite the tearing down of employment barriers, these tendencies still exist. Most construction workers are men. Most social workers are women. The military is predominantly male. Office workers predominantly female.

Fashion sense is clearly a cultural phenomenon, but one that the genders take seriously.

Studies show that men and women tend to think differently as well. It is said that men think more objectively, while women employ more of an intuitive subjectivity. Both have great value, and the species is stronger for having them.

Certain physical and child raising instincts differ as might be expected because of nature's influence in procreation.

Sexual interest recognizes obvious differences. Even homosexuality is based on differentiated preferences.

In nature, among a thousand separate species, gender differences are obvious and well-documented. We recognize their value and are amazed at their symbiotic creativity.

We know all these facts, yet our fear of being branded as sexist makes us shy away from them. Is it right to do this? Or are we basing our decisions on just a different form of sexism, one that refuses to recognize differences because they are viewed with different value? Does sexism lie at the heart of our timidity and denial? This is one of the reasons why the Sixth Trust tells us to refute sexism in all its guises. In our desire to fight the good fight, we have to become mindful of sexist tendencies we might not be aware of.

There is a difference between equality and homogeneity. Men and women are equal because they represent two valid and necessary genders of the same human race. Whatever generalized differences that exist should not place them in critical competition. The success of our species depends on them both. For the most part, these differences are complementary, but not necessarily exclusive. Each gender exhibits traits of the other. Sometimes it is just a statistical matter of proportion. Nevertheless, to deny these tendencies is to deny simple truth.

The second principle, *respecting the female gender* as a whole, makes absolute sense to the man of chivalry. That humanity expresses itself in two separate and complementary genders, it is right for each to appreciate the other, thereby better enabling a positive partnership. It is quite as simple as that. We can refer to this as *transpersonal respect*.

This is where chivalry asserts that proper courtesy should be exhibited by men toward women. It does not articulate how women should respond in return. As a male ethic, it would not be appropriate. Women have every right to decide their own ethics for themselves.

Unfortunately, chivalric courtesy toward women has been disparaged as of late by women who incorrectly translate any hint of preferential deference as an insult, and men who are afraid of being regarded as sexist.

Here we find ourselves in a serious dilemma. Courtesy toward women lies at the heart of chivalry, and always has. To those who own just a superficial idea of this code of ethics, such courtesy is what chivalry is all about. Mention the word, and one immediately thinks of opening doors for ladies — a constant focus of discussion and dissention. Some of our Companions defend themselves by saying that they open doors for both sexes, as if courtesy toward women, by itself, was something questionable.

How should today's chivalry respond to this? Can it recognize and honor gender differences without being charged with inherent sexism? Or has feminist caution and hypersensitive political correctness made this impossible?

***

To start with, as men, we need to recognize women's humanity as individuals first, who, like all of us, have their own unique characteristics. It is plain to see that most women are complex, intelligent, and compassionate persons, deserving of our respect and friendship. They are not perfect, and it is wrong to expect them to be. As individuals, they are not put on this earth to cater to the needs or preferences of men. That they differ from males should not be seen as a source of contention, but as something that offers tremendous possibilities for partnership. Individual differences have to be respected as well. Not every woman is right for partnership with every man. Not every man is right for every woman. What could be more apparent than that? Partnership demands compatibility and a certain amount of negotiation. Each partner's perspective should be a valid concern for them both.

Some women, as is true for some men, might not deserve respect. This sentiment should come only after suitable judgment can be made, never as a prejudgment. Respectful, courteous communication begins the process of acquaintance, and opinions form naturally from there.

***

Our culture has long been blighted from a history of prejudice and discrimination. Victims have included people of color, various ethnicities, different sexual orientations, religious differences, and gender. While most of these prejudices have been aimed at minority populations, originating in ignorance and distrust, this is not true for women, who are present throughout every society and generally outnumber men.

Matters of race, religion, ethnicity and sexual preference often raise the kind of fear and tribal consciousness that come from a lack of familiarity. People feel threatened by what they do not understand.

In comparison, sexual discrimination is unique. Women have always been a vital part of our households and communities. They usually shared the same religious beliefs and culture. Men are raised and are familiar with women from birth. As children, both genders play together. As adults, they work together. They share special intimacies and solemn commitments. They experience each other's joys and tragedies, and raise children together.

Men naturally love women as wives, sisters, mothers, friends and co-workers.

How is it that these same men feel free to dominate them and cheat them of their rights? Abuse them physically and emotionally? Devalue their opinions? Ignore their feelings? Disregard their talents? Trivialize their interests? Use coercion to possess them as objects? Offer lower wages and less challenging employment? Cheapen their sexuality through commercialism and entertainment?

Any fair minded person knows full well that this is wrong, and has to shut off something of his conscience in order to partake in it.

Gender discrimination reflects a thoughtless, insidious dis-respect that is endemic in a culture where both genders are closely established and familiar with one another. Ignorance remains part of it, of course, but it is an ignorance that is system-atically taught and sustained as part of a broken culture.

Gender represents a powerful grouping instinct that is based on sexuality and traditional gender roles, neither of which can be erased or easily ignored. Men and women are physically different from one another, and those differences have intrinsic meaning to the survival of the species. That these differences should imply inequality favorable to prejudice and oppression simply does not make sense.

The problem we face today is one that has not been well thought out. To eliminate sexual discrimination, which is a worthy goal, should we attack the core problem by eradicating differences? Some think this is a viable course, no matter how contrary to nature and freedom it is.

A more sensible approach is this. It is the nature of freedom and equality for people to retain whatever individual differences they enjoy as part of their pursuit of happiness. Men do not have to stop being men in order to support women's equality and civil rights. Likewise, women do not have to stop being women in order to be considered equal.

What we need to assure gender equality is to honor and respect basic differences for what they are.

This is not a matter of skin color, religion or ethnicity. It is a matter of biology and cultural acclimation. Ignoring genuine differences is just as bad as disparaging them, if not worse, resulting in the worst kind of insult and social engineering.

The richness acquired through gender differences is vital to our existence and understanding of the world, and contributes to the strength and versatility of our species. Civilization has always maintained a combination of both.

Recognizing and honoring differences is probably the most effective weapon we have against sexism. It offers no impediments to gender relations at all, but facilitates their advancement through fairness, courtesy and respect.

What do women say? One female visitor to our web site said this:

"Think of Chivalry-Now as the counterpart of the feminism movement, a philosophical partner that heals the wounds of the male gender, just as feminism heals the wounds of women."

Another said:

"I'm a life-long feminist. I make no bones about it... Chivalry-Now is taking responsibility for the man's part in the exploration and improvement of gender relations. How could I not be interested?"

While these comments do not speak for all women, they reflect the sentiments of fair-minded feminists who understand what Chivalry-Now is trying to do.

***

What follows is a surprisingly enlightened medieval tale relevant to our discussion, *The Wedding of Gawain and Ragnall.*

It begins with King Arthur being challenged, on pain of death, to find the answer to a question within one year's time. The question was this: *what do women want most?*

As the year went by, King Arthur asked everyone he met for their opinion. Some suggested that what women wanted most was flattery, others suggested a relentless lover, or a new gown or favorite pet. The king considered all these answers, but none seemed appropriate.

Continuing his search, he came across a hideously distorted, frightfully homely old woman who eagerly confronted him. Her name was Ragnall. She claimed to have the answer that he sought, but would not tell him unless the king promised her the hand of Sir Gawain, his nephew. Now, Gawain was a young, handsome knight, known throughout the land for his courtesy and prowess. Arthur refused to command this of his nephew, but agreed to tell him, which he did. The loyal Gawain, ever ready to sacrifice himself for a worthy cause, agreed to marry Ragnall in order to save his uncle's life. Ragnall then revealed the answer to King Arthur:

"What women want is sovereignty over their own lives," she declared, *"the power to be free even over men."*

When Arthur heard this, he knew that it was true. By providing this answer, he was spared from death on his day of reckoning.

Sir Gawain was not so fortunate. He had to marry Ragnall as promised, with a huge wedding for all to see.

On their wedding night, a strange thing happened. Gawain turned to find that Ragnall had magically transformed herself into the fairest woman he had ever seen.

Ragnall explained that a curse had been put upon her, and the transformation was limited to half the hours of every day. She asked him which half he preferred to see her beautiful, day or night? By day, everyone would admire his wife. By night, their love-making would be that more pleasurable.

Gawain told her he could not decide. It was her decision to make, much like the answer of sovereignty she had given to the king. Ragnall smiled. Because of his response, the curse upon her was broken and she became beautiful all the time.

This tale carries a lesson surprisingly enlightened for the times in which it was written. King Arthur, for instance, considered Ragnall's answer obviously true, and yet no one other than Ragnall came up with it during that entire year. Answers to problems are often right before us, plain in sight, and we fail to see them.

Sir Gawain's response shows that proper chivalry tells us to honor women in their totality, as free agents over their own lives. Not just accept that view, or give modicum respect, but honor its value, protect it as we would our own, and never turn against it.

This is especially true in matters of love, where each partner cherishes the well-being of the other. This is not to say that sacrifices will not be made to the relationship by both parties. What it means is that sacrifices should be fair and willingly given as free expressions of love.

***

Chivalry tells us that we should honor and respect women, and we have every reason to do so. Nothing is more obvious than the appreciation we owe them as our partners, mothers, sisters, friends and fellow human beings. Their vision of the world continually enriches our own when we allow ourselves to listen.

So far, as a male ethic, chivalry shows itself to be an honest broker in respecting the rights of both sexes. But medieval chivalry went one step further, obligating knights to not only honor *all* women, but to *serve* them as well.

Serve?

To our modern sensibilities, that runs somewhat against the grain. Freedom, yes. Equality, of course. Servitude? Not likely. It hardly suits the independent temperament of modern society. To better understand this requirement, we need to look back to its beginnings.

During medieval times, Christianity had a profound social influence that is difficult to imagine today. Its teachings permeated everything, from the calendar, where each day memorialized a saint, to a flattened *terra firma* sandwiched between heaven and hell, where angels, devils and even dragons were thought to be real. Life was often so difficult that only the promise of an afterlife of eternal joy carried them through.

The times were not only religious, they were also violent, often pitting one neighboring city against another. The Church did its best to subdue this. It taught peace and brotherly love, and strongly condemned the sin of pride. It went so far as to link itself with chivalry. Clerics transformed knighthood into a sacred rite, where the knighting ceremony was administered in a church or chapel, rather than on the battlefield.

One of the quotes from the bible that gave hope to the impoverished majority of this stratified society was this: *the first shall be last, and the last first.*

This seemed to challenge the natural order of the world, where the strong and powerful gained far more privileges than the average peasant. It offered dignity and hope to those who were poor, while also serving as a warning to those in power. Punishment and reward in the afterlife would compensate for inequities here on earth.

The New Testament confirmed this in no uncertain terms, coming from Jesus himself:

"You know that the rulers of the Gentiles lord it over them, and their high officials exercise authority over them. Not so with you. Instead, whoever wants to be great among you must be your *servant*, and whoever wants to be first must be your *slave* — just as the Son of Man did not come to be served, but *to serve*..." (Matt. 10:28)

There was that word again. The concept was not lost after Jesus. The apostle Paul continued in that vein:

"You, my brothers, were called to be free. But do not use your *freedom* to indulge the sinful nature; rather, *serve* one another in love." (Gal. 5:13)

This last quote connects the ideas of *freedom* and *service* in an interesting way. It says that freedom should not be used to indulge what it calls the *sinful nature*.

From our perspective it means this: real freedom starts only when we express the authenticity of our *original nature*. Once that authenticity is attained, true freedom becomes the expression of real self.

Likewise, a real commitment can only be made by someone who makes it freely.

When we freely serve others it is an act of love. Mothers reflect this in the care they show their children. So too, the child who takes care of an ailing parent. You see it in friendships, patriotism, business loyalties, kindness toward neighbors, and courtesy for strangers. There is beauty in this giving because it is not mandated or imposed by others. It comes from our deepest nature. This is not servitude or slavery in the modern sense of unwilling toil. The willingness of the act, and the love it instigates, is nothing less than a shared abundance of life itself.

This liberation frees us not only from social expectations, but from our egos as well. English cleric Thomas Fuller (1654-1743) said it best:

"Serving one's own passions is the greatest slaver."

True freedom is the expression of our inner selves unshackled by convention. It produces acts of kindness that Jesus, Paul the apostle, and spiritual leaders from around the world have long recognized as our greatest goal.

Such compassion exemplifies worldly and spiritual love at its finest. It becomes a spontaneous part of who we are when we are really ourselves.

Like many spiritual truths, the willingness to serve others turns conventional wisdom upside down. In a world rife with violence, the strong are obviously in a position to rule the weak. But Jesus pointed to something different: *Blessed are the meek...* And blessed they are — along with the peacemakers, and those who show mercy and are pure in heart. These are the people who heal the world, rather than harm it. This is the power of *humility* (see Chapter 6).

You don't have to be religious to appreciate this. These are qualities of the ideal knight, qualities already available within ourselves.

By *serving women* we mean affording them every respect while taking the initiative to work with them as their natural partners. We do this as men, providing our own male virtues to support mutual civilizing goals. We bring something special, just as they bring something special.

The combination strengthens us all.

***

Female virtues are just as important to society as male virtues — perhaps more so, considering the part they play in procreation and the civilizing influences of women. As honorable men, it would be remiss not to honor womanhood itself, inclusive of all women, young and old, of every race and creed. Anything less detracts from our overall commitment. We do this when we courteously anticipate the worth of every woman we meet, and only withdraw that respect if the woman proves herself unworthy.

Today, the popular concept of chivalry has been reduced to courtesies toward women which we consider those of a gentleman. These outward courtesies include:

Opening doors for women, giving up seats for them on a crowded bus, helping to carry their packages or school books, speaking to them politely, treating them with care.

To be genuine, however, courtesy toward women includes much more. It includes seeing them as equals, listening to them with interest and an open mind, respecting their wishes and opinions, being there for them when needed, accepting them as friends in the complete sense of the word, keeping your commitments, purifying your capacity for love, protecting their interests as your partners in life, and being the best partner you can be.

If outward courtesies do not reflect these inner qualities, they are false and usually come with a price — which is not chivalry, but something crass and manipulative. Sincerity is essential to chivalrous behavior, and women should have no doubt that your words and actions are sincere.

However you express your courtesy towards women, you should never imply that you do so because she is weaker than a man, or less competent in any capacity, or has incurred a debt for your assistance. Do it out of respect alone, and a sense of politeness. Anything less is an act of demeaning arrogance, and women would have every right to resent you. Courtesy must never be seen as asserting dominance as sometimes happened in the past. Humility is either genuine, or it is prideful. No in-between.

If you have doubts about women's strength and abilities, consider how they survived centuries of brutal oppression from unenlightened males and still performed heroically to protect their loved ones and contribute to the making of a better world. In some cultures, they manage to survive degradation and persecution even today. This speaks volumes on behalf of the character and determination of women. I wonder how men would fare in similar circumstances.

***

There is nothing more opposite to chivalry, or any other viable concept of manhood, than treating women poorly and without proper respect. Abusing women is a malevolence that shames not only the men who perpetrate such deeds, but those who fail to denounce them as well. There can be no excuse for all the gender related crimes that happen today, other than a blight upon manhood for allowing it.

Stalking, wife-beating and rape are nearly endemic in our society, and in much of the world. In the workplace, we find sexual discrimination and the so-called invisible ceiling. Rap music has introduced some of the most vile portrayals of women that have ever been heard. Pornographers flourish in our society as so-called honest business people by portraying women in degrading ways. There are places in the world that actually condone the suppression of women's rights, segregation, restrictive education, cloaking women's faces so they cannot be seen, female infanticide, and ritualized murder of rape victims. There are families that sell their daughters into slavery and prostitution. Sweatshops bordering on concentration camps. Terrorist strategies of rape and mutilation.

Perpetrators include sports celebrities, successful businessmen, diplomats, talented artists, performers, religious preachers, clerics, and other citizens who otherwise are considered upstanding. No matter what façade they hide behind, truth reveals them to be broken, pathetic creatures disconnected from the very core of their own moral values.

Today's chivalry must stand up and condemn all these actions in the strongest terms. It calls for each of us to look into the darkness of our souls for any vestiges of angry sexism that we can find and weed it out.

By restoring healthy idealism back into our own culture, we can do a better job in combating misogyny. It is up to each of us to renew our goals, hold higher beliefs and commit ourselves to a world where manhood can claim the virtues that it should be synonymous with.

It is possible to build a new Camelot where everyone can enjoy equal rights and a sense of safety. That means building it in ourselves first. When we do that, our larger goals are that much closer.

***

Is there a feminine side to chivalry?

It is important to recognize that the virtues of chivalry are not in any way exclusively male. How could they be? Moral values like truth, justice and mercy are not determined by gender. They are values in and of themselves that any person can appreciate.

What might appear to be exclusive is the way in which men accept, validate and express these values in their lives.

In a sense, chivalry belongs to men because it was formed to reflect the warrior spirit of males. In general terms, it expresses the best of who we are as men, and does this by appealing to the male psyche. Indeed, Chivalry-Now can be considered a remedy to our culture's lack of social acclimation for men. It does this as a male code of ethics.

Although women may respond to the same values in their own way, which should be determined by them alone, chivalry is a warrior code designed for men alone. If it were not, it would lose some of its influence on this target population, which has such need for it.

This is not to say that women cannot partake or value what chivalry espouses. The quest is open to us all, and rewards anyone who takes it with new life and authenticity. I think many women partake in their own quests already, and I encourage them to listen to their own warrior spirit to guide them.

Today's chivalry provides a prescription for what ails the male psyche, and the symptoms that this ailment propagates throughout society. As mentioned earlier, it is the counterpart of feminism, where each approach positively impacts everyone by uniquely focusing on a specific gender.

A woman cannot give birth to a man. The man has to do that for himself, in the context of his culture. She can certainly help, but a man's spiritual birth can only arise from his own striving.

Chivalry provides the blueprint to make that happen. It was meant to build and guide men according to their own perspective. It offers the spiritual rite-of-passage that men need. If women understand how chivalry provides this, they will understand the purpose of its focus.

Can a woman become a knight errant? Why not?

That being said, whatever code they follow should be theirs to formulate so that it reflects their own perspective. This would also give them a sense of ownership of their code.

The question of a feminine side to chivalry leads to an important issue that needs to be discussed.

Modern psychology has accomplished miracles of the mind for countless people. The pioneers of this science leave us much to be grateful for. There is one fashionable idea in psychology that I take contention with, despite my admiration for it. The idea that there is a *feminine side* to men, while valid in many of its assumptions, leads to what I feel is a powerful error.

Something very important is lost when the gentler qualities of manhood are translated as belonging to another sex. For one thing, it hardens the image of the male psyche as something two dimensional. Indeed, it promotes resistance in men to many of their own impulses.

It is wrong to assume that men have or need an *inner woman* to complete themselves. To say that we do infers that the gentler aspects of men do not reflect manhood at all, but those of another sex that have infiltrated their psyches.

As revealing and helpful to our understanding as an inner woman concept is, in the end it denies the full range of qualities that are specifically male.

When a man feels compassion and tenderness, when he

cuddles a child, or weeps in sadness, these responses should not be viewed as coming from some hidden female counterpart. He is reflecting the range of his own feelings and should embrace them as such. Why should it not be possible for men to be loving, attentive and gentle and still be 100% male? Anything less makes our concept of manhood so pathetically shallow that we encourage our culture to reject us as knaves and miscreants. What we need to do is recognize the obvious: these qualities are our own. They are part of us as men.

Just because a man hesitates to reveal his emotions does not mean he does not feel them.

That we convince ourselves otherwise shows how fragile our self-image can be. I strongly object to anyone who tells me that my feelings spring from a source other than who I am as a complete man. There is no inner woman peeking out. That these qualities resemble qualities of women only proves our commonality. Both genders breathe to live and eat when hungry. Both experience a full range of feelings as well.

When a woman is strong and honorable, she is not exhibiting male characteristics, as if women cannot otherwise be strong and honorable. She is who she is, a strong and noble woman. She does not need an inner man telling her how to be so.

When men are in touch with their depth of humanity, they find a rich variety of responses to the world that include love and sensitivity. By nature or nurture, they may express it in different ways than women, or have different priorities, but their responses are real and belong to them as men.

When males search to define themselves as men, they naturally resist recognizing a "feminine side" to their personality. It suggests that their masculinity is incomplete by nature. Asking them to adopt a *feminine side* to their personality is not a viable answer. Discovering their own true depth and range of possibilities as men seems far more direct and reasonable.

Chivalry-Now encourages men to incorporate their full range

of male qualities, strong and gentle, in order to discover and partake in their own authenticity.

There is nothing unmanly about showing affection to the woman we love, and yet some men think that it is. When I treat my wife with tenderness, I am more of a man than if I were incapable of doing so.

Chivalry-Now calls upon men to take full ownership of their depth of character, and provides the means to do this.

***

In consideration of the Sixth Trust, we should not be surprised when some feminists misconstrue our intent. It does well to remember that feminism has fought a long and difficult war against an entrenched power structure that historically treated women with fewer rights and privileges, lower wages, and hidden contempt. That war continues.

Women have a right to look upon anything that calls itself a male ethic with suspicion. Men should too, for that matter. If what we say is true, it should hold up to any scrutiny.

Chivalry-Now is not an attempt to reinstate male dominance in today's society. It calls for equality and recognition that men are partners of women. It accepts and approves of the goals of feminism wholeheartedly.

That Chivalry-Now focuses on the psychological needs of males by providing a sorely needed code of ethics should not be viewed as something wrong or threatening to women. We hope it is quite the opposite. By healing the wounds of men, just as feminism heals those of women, we look forward to a better world for all.

Men who are sufficiently inspired by Chivalry-Now will not be predators, or dominators, or devalue a woman's labor. They will assist with household chores, and show affection more freely. They will help to raise children and model what it means to be a proper man. They will not be obnoxiously aggressive, and will feel free enough to enjoy compassion in their lives. They will develop their skills knowing that self-improvement increases their capabilities to create and sustain a better world. Best of all, nature will have its due — they will do this as who they are, as men, honoring strength and justice for all.

When confronted by women who question our motives, we must be patient with their concerns, and do our best to prove ourselves worthy of their trust. Just as feminism has been distorted and victimized by fear and misunderstanding, Chivalry-Now may be so as well. As women have shown themselves strong and resilient, we will do the same.

I admire the accomplishments of feminism. In certain respects, they have achieved a degree of *personal* liberation that men have yet to dream of.

Chapter 10

"Upholding Justice…"

Trust # 7: I will uphold justice by being fair to all.

Justice plays an important role in any cultural ethic. It is related to power in that power without justice is morally incomplete; it becomes wild and destructive, like tyrants and hurricanes. History shows us time and again that unbridled power held by the few is the quickest path to ruin for any society. It is equally ruinous to personal relationships.

The trouble is, power without justice can lead to quick and easy profit. This is why people commit crimes, on the streets and in the boardroom. The reward seems to outweigh the risk.

From the perspective of chivalry, justice provides us with the sole validation for power. Strength is measured not only by the size of one's muscles, but by the purpose it is dedicated to serve. Moral ethics cannot condone the abuse of power. Strength is wasted unless it serves a good cause. This is where justice comes in, revealing a path of fairness and moral action.

Justice helps uphold the other principles of the Twelve Trusts, such as defining one's character, defending those who cannot defend themselves, and resisting all forms of discrimination. In our relationships, justice promotes generosity and takes no pleasure in scandal. It means treating people fairly, from which courtesy arises. Justice is related to truth in that one often relies upon the other. It allows for mercy, as only justice can.

***

During the Middle Ages, chivalry's meting out of justice sometimes resulted in the clash of swords, an image that has been popularized in movies and novels. Another infamous example was that of punishing a man for killing the king's deer by chopping off his hand.

Historically, such punishments were not common. A judicial system existed and was applied fairly (to cases of theft of the king's deer at least, less fairly to charges of witchcraft, where thousands of innocent women were killed for such offenses as simple as growing herbs). Chopping off hands, branding faces, whippings and hangings — while real and horrible punishments — served more as a deterrent than an actual sentence. There was good reason for that. First of all, the judicial system required strong evidence which had to be presented at the trial, which might occur months after the crime. Dead deer were not easy to preserve; witnesses not easy to gather.

On top of that, the judge or magistrate could extend mercy, which he often did. In a feudal society, survival of the realm depended on the contributions of the many. It was not economical to maim, cripple or execute supporting vassals. It also depleted the pool of able bodied manpower needed for defense.

It was a different world back then. People were valued more for what they produced than for how greedily they consumed, which is how our value system rewards us now. Our population is so large today that we do not even consider the loss of productive citizens who are imprisoned. Most of them are men who have lost their way. Not that I am advocating their release without suitable rehabilitation. I merely find the number of men who get themselves incarcerated both astounding and shameful. What was missing from their lives that determined such consequences? Is it missing from ours as well?

Our system of justice is not less humane than the system of the Middle Ages. What remains lacking is a true sense of justice, a desire to make things right. We see guilty parties released from custody as if they did nothing wrong. We see criminals who committed heinous crimes get early release for good behavior. We see men who abuse women or children return to the community where they continue to abuse them. We see millions of dollars spent on high profile cases, while the poor are hardly represented at all. People from ethnic minorities tend to get harsher sentences. Despite all our efforts and best intentions, real justice is scarce.

Our system is rarely just and fails to change things for the better. When young offenders are incarcerated with hardened criminals, they learn the ways of those criminals in order to survive among them – and often become worse criminals upon release. The rate of recidivism bears this out. Studies taken in 1994 showed that 67% of criminals released in the United States offended again and were re-incarcerated within three years.

Is there a better way? Probably not. What system could possibly deal with so many people in a systematic, rehabilitative manner? Prisons are overcrowded. The system is cumbersome, inefficient, expensive, and fraught with loopholes for the wealthy.

The truth is, justice cannot be found in any judicial system. To find it, we need to look elsewhere. Justice is a moral value that either exists in people, or it does not exist at all. By the time an offender is in custody awaiting trial, moral justice has already failed. What awaits is a judicial contest followed by punishment or acquittal. We miss the point entirely.

Chivalry-Now approaches this problem where it starts — *culturally* — by bringing the concept of justice to the forefront of people's minds. If people thought more about justice in their everyday lives, and expressed it by its corollary, fairness, our world would instantly change for the better. It all starts with our vision of the world and the way we treat other people.

Simply put, when we *believe* in justice and incorporate it into our lives, we don't lie or cheat or steal. We don't commit violent crimes. We abhor prejudice and discrimination. When we accidently hurt someone, we feel remorse and willingly make amends by offering generous compensation.

***

Chivalry-Now recommends a very different approach to our social problems. There can be no morally comprehensive solutions to problems apart from us, the people who bring morality to life. Rules and commandments are only words. Our response to them makes them real. Morality exists only in us, and culture helps to make that happen.

Expensive programs that try to compensate for social deprivations can only go so far. Restraining people by law and punishment may regulate behavior up to a point, but only at the failure of the culture's heart and soul. Culture is an agreed upon set of shared values that imbues our collective conscience with common ground. When these values support community as well as personal interests, the improvements are self-perpetuating. When they are missing or contradictory, or when we feel excluded from them, other values take their place, such as the all-pervasive greed we see today.

Mending our culture is not the same as *social engineering*. Culture develops within us and distills itself from a long history of human relations already rooted in who we are.

***

Justice is related to our concept of freedom. Freedom without justice, without a strong sense of what is right and good, does not produce the personal liberation that authenticity requires. It produces chaos.

Freedom means lack of restraint. On one level, the ability to do as one chooses; on another level, a government that does not oppress its people. It means equal protection under the law, and a system whereby people decide their own fate.

On a deeper, more immediate level, freedom makes serious demands upon us all. While it provides the opportunity to act freely, it depends upon a liberation of thought as well. Anything less is incomplete. It is this liberation of thought that holds the greatest potential for freedom, one that is capable of transforming the entire world.

It is right to expect grand achievements from people who are free. If we look around us and see personal malaise, apathy and moral stagnation, we can be sure that the energies and inspirations of freedom have somehow been lost.

These propensities are symptomatic of a culture that fails to inspire what is best in its citizens.

Having the world's largest economy is not the truest measure of national success. The truest measure of success is the quality of people's lives. Not how wealthy they are, how many cars they own, or where they go on vacation, but who they are as moral individuals.

The intent of justice is to make this kind of freedom possible by imbuing it with responsibility. When responsibility lessens, freedom becomes nothing more than misdirected license, and a burden on our judicial system.

Personal liberation comes to life when we *freely* and consistently choose to do what our *liberated moral center* tells us is right.

This is not some lofty idea that springs from Chivalry-Now alone. Freedom and justice have been recognized goals throughout the ages. Prophets cried out for it. Peasants rose up against unjust rulers. Nations split. Martyrs can be found in every society in the world.

Liberation from self, or ego, can be found in some of the great mystical traditions. In the East, we find Buddhist and Hindu philosophies. In the West, we find Stoicism, Transcendentalism and contemplative religious traditions.

The differences between these regional philosophies are striking. In the East, liberation of self aims more at liberation *from* self, which is formalized through rigorous meditation discipline. Practitioners focus on releasing ego attachments, escaping the cycle of earthly reincarnation, or finding release from the senses in order to avoid pain and sorrow. It concentrates on silence, calm and withdrawal — the nothingness of Tao or Nirvana. This is presented less severely in the Middle Way of Buddhism.

In the West, liberation of self means the discipline to put our ego behind us, and respond to the world more directly by doing so. It is life-engaging, participatory, morally progressive, rather than passively accepting. We search for greater truth in the Mystery of things, and greater experience of life itself. Our efforts concentrate on understanding and tapping into the personal energy of discovery — the fullness of living in the moment with abundant life.

This is nothing new. Consider the following:

– *Johann Wolfgang von Goethe*, German poet, dramatist and philosopher.
"None are more hopelessly enslaved than those who falsely believe that they are free."

– *William Ellery Channing*, 18th century American Unitarian minister.
"The only freedom worth possessing is that which gives enlargement to a people's energy, intellect, and virtues... Progress, the growth of intelligence and power, is the end and boon of liberty; and, without this, a people may have the name, but want the substance and spirit of freedom."

– *David Garrick*, 18th century English actor and dramatist,
"Corrupted freemen are the worst of slaves."

– *Albert Einstein*, German scientist.
"The true value of a human being is determined by the measure and the sense in which he has attained liberation from the self."

– *William Cowper*, 18th century poet.
"He is the freeman whom *the truth makes free*, and all are slaves beside."

It is this Western tradition that best describes the goals of Chivalry-Now.

***

Honoring justice in our lives provides a moral foundation that we can count on. It comes from treating others the way we want to be treated —what we commonly call the *Golden Rule*. Here we find basic social morality, the foundation of law and human rights that form the moral directives for both religion and humanism. This simple concept is capable of uniting us all.

Justice is found in the way we treat one another: polite, friendly, and concerned enough with everyone's well-being, including our own, to be fair in all our dealings. This sets the tone for just relationships. In a world where courtesy flourishes, injustice does not occur without immediate recompense. Courtesy, like justice, means doing the right thing.

Unfortunately, things seem to be going in the opposite direction. Thanks to media trends and the outrage of talk radio, civility and courtesy is being replaced by coarseness, vulgarity and outright lies. If fairness and truth are no longer the mainstream of popular discourse, can justice long survive?

***

A powerful impediment to justice comes from our capacity to indulge conflicting values. Our obsession with wealth and power contradicts the more austere ideologies that spring from Stoic and Judeo-Christian traditions. Despite this obvious conflict, we continue to pay homage to them both, which has a direct impact on our priorities in life, our social conscience, and the way we treat one another.

The Christian Gospel warns about this in no uncertain terms:

- *You cannot serve both God and Mammon (money).*
- *A house divided must fall.*
- *It is easier for a rich person to pass through the eye of a needle than to enter the Kingdom of Heaven.*

I can think of nothing that Jesus condemned more than the trappings of wealth and power, other than the religious hypocrisy that supports them both.

Chivalry-Now tells us that it is time to reaffirm what we already know.

Greed is immoral.

Greed is not the same as receiving decent compensation for one's labor. It is not vying for a promotion that you well deserve. It is not providing a comfortable home for your family, or saving money for your children's education or your personal retirement.

Greed is an obsessive dissatisfaction that makes us want more and more money, more things that are well beyond our means, to the point of turning our backs on the welfare of others. Greed is also found in the craving for more and more power.

We see examples of this everywhere we look:

- When the barometer of our day is decided by the rise and fall of the stock market.
- When we behave ruthlessly at work or in our careers, knifing people in the back to get a promotion.
- When we hear about the dangers of global warming and

do nothing about it.

- When we are willing to discard the well-being of our neighbors and fellow citizens in order to avoid higher taxes.
- When we lie or cheat to increase our wealth or power.
- When we send jobs overseas, disregarding the employment needs of our own people and the working conditions of foreign factories.
- When we hide our immoral acts behind the aegis of corporate interests.
- When political leaders use fear to manipulate us to increase their power.
- When religion is misused to generate personal wealth and greater control.

Greed comes sharply into play when people mean less to us than money or power or that new house.

When people around the world look to us for moral leadership, it only increases our culpability.

We are basically a loving, caring people. How is it that for the sake of increased profitability we are taught not to care about something as vital to our collective survival and well-being as the environment? How is it that we ignore the cost of innocent casualties of war just to regard ourselves as victorious? How can we turn a blind eye when our most sacred and moral imperatives are twisted to achieve personal ambitions? How is it that we raise the banner of freedom in the world and not expect to be held to a higher standard?

There is a reason. A very simple one. We are only human, and for some time now we have lost our way.

The responsibilities of freedom are weighty and constant. They demand a code of ethics not imposed from without but inspired from within. This philosophical mandate is in no way contrary to freedom. Self-discipline is the very essence of freedom. It gives us the control over our actions that makes freedom possible. If there is anything we can learn from chivalry, it should be that.

***

Justice can never be found by the whip, sword, or punishments of the magistrate or law. The function of law is to punish violators. Such power is exerted only when justice fails.

If you wish to find justice, seek it in what is fair and true. The virtue of justice is meant to protect us all.

Live rightly and justice abounds.

Chapter 11

"Faithful in Love..."

Trust # 8: I will be faithful in love and loyal in friendship.

Faithfulness and loyalty are fundamental attributes of every true knight. Without these qualities, knighthood is meaningless. The same applies to our definition of manhood.

Faithfulness and loyalty speak volumes about personal character. They determine how we relate to other people, including our friends, family and spouse. Here we find the everyday ingredients of chivalry at work, the intimate give-and-take of our principles. If faithfulness and loyalty are not a prominent part of who we are and how we treat people, then the essence of chivalry escapes our efforts.

Both of these qualities are reflections of love, which supersede all other values as the final measure of a man. Love shapes us more than anything else. It reflects our interests, our values, our personal worth. It provides the kind of pleasure and agony that fills our lives with the immediacy of living.

Considering how important love is, and how much of our lives are affected by it, one would think we would own a concise definition of what it is.

A significant amount of our economy depends on love's illusions. Songs celebrate love. Religion extols its importance. Love novels fill the bookshelves, and movies include it in almost all their plots. When we try to define it, however, the words remain wanting.

To understand love, we need to comprehend that it involves more than just a feeling, emotion or instinct.

As we defined the word *spiritual* in an earlier chapter, love is more than the sum of its parts. Human consciousness elevates instinct and emotion to an entirely new and unique level. This is why we often use words like destiny, soul-mates and eternity when we speak about love. They suggest something that transcends physical instinct because that is how we encounter it. Love is spiritual, and we proclaim it as such.

This connection is so strong that the Bible declares that *God is love* (1 John 4:16). This scriptural quotation, more than any other, helped liberate the romantic love of chivalry from the strict rules of medieval convention. It gave people new license to approach God without an intermediary, through something as simple as what moves the heart. If love provides direct access to God, perhaps faith can be as direct as well. This may have challenged Church authority enough to make the Protestant Revolution possible.

Once again we find the tenets of chivalry offering deeper meaning than is obvious.

***

When the writer of *1 John* equated God with love, he inspired new vistas of thought that pointed to love as the highest *religious impulse* there is:

Love is the most *personal*. It affirms the individual as someone capable of love, while affirming the worth of his or her beloved.

It is also the *most real and direct* spiritual impulse. It is not transubstantiation. It is not an ancient relic or ritual. It is not praying into the silence hoping to be heard, or nurturing guilt that disaffirms the very life we would otherwise enjoy. It is a direct experience of spiritual joy.

- Love flourishes on *truth*. Romantic love, despite its roman-
  ticized image, actually requires the shedding of illusions.
  Each person becomes completely revealed, good and bad,

during the process of intimacy. This experience touches the mystery of life itself and makes it transcendent.

- Love is an *impulse toward union.* If God is love, than the union it begets is nothing less than partaking in the impetus of God in our daily lives.
- Love makes spirituality *tangible.* It makes worship real.
- Love is a daily *sacrifice* of self to a relationship, through which both parties give and mutually benefit. In this way, the two become one.
- Love brings *new life* into the world, and in this respect, it is life itself.
- Love includes *faith* in that other person, and *hope* for the future.
- Love's *spiritual intensity* can be likened to contemplative prayer.
- We access *joy* from its levity, life from its beauty, security from its steadfastness, and tenacity from its enduring quality.
- Most mysterious of all, in moments of serene quiet, we discover the *sublime.*

All people had to do was look inside themselves to find their direct connection to God. This simple realization seemed far more authentic than rules, sacraments or rituals.

***

The inclusion of romantic love makes chivalry unique as a warrior code. This should come as no surprise. As a male ethic, chivalry would be incomplete without attending to matters of the heart.

Romantic love gave rise to its medieval counterpart, *courtly love,* which became a fashionable diversion among the nobility. Almost a game, it had rules, prizes, winners and losers. Judging by the literature, it was sometimes taken seriously, as games of love often are.

A combination of sport, elite-gamesmanship and risk-taking, courtly love challenged one of the traditional fixtures of early medieval society: arranged marriages.

It was long customary in medieval Europe, as it was elsewhere in the world, for parents to choose their children's future spouses at an early age. For the commoner, this often meant betrothals between friends or neighbors, or distant relatives. Among the aristocracy, arrangements were based on political and family alliances, with much the same results.

Even though the prospective couple might not be acquainted with each other, after they married they accepted their respective roles. The arrangement was sanctioned by church and state, which considered such marriages the fabric of society.

Marriage was not looked upon as an institution based on love. It was a familial obligation designed to produce children, which would hopefully bring security to old age. This is not to say that arranged marriages excluded love. It was expected that affection would develop over time. Without free choice by the individuals concerned, however, the lifetime commitment sometimes led to resentment. To make matters worse, arranged marriages did not stop people from falling in love with other people — setting the stage for moral conflict.

These were the *family values* issues of their day, colliding squarely with a growing, controversial sense of personal and emotional autonomy.

***

Christian contact with Muslims during the Crusades intro-duced Islamic poetry into Western culture. These poems often expressed a man's longing for a woman who was beyond his reach. Troubadours incorporated this theme into songs and poetry of their own. This spark eventually rekindled the Western fire of individuality that was practically annihilated with the fall of Rome, and now contended with the status quo.

The basic premise of courtly love was that personal attraction was spontaneous and natural, and had value of its own that deserved to be honored. The *idea* of destiny and of love at first sight became obsessive.

One might assume that this resulted in people wanting to marry someone they fell in love with, but that was not the case. Marriage was so solidly defined by family arrangement that romantic love assigned itself to the excitement of extra-marital relationships. There were those who insisted that a husband and wife were naturally barred from sharing such love. Romantic love could therefore be achieved only by those who were unmarried or through adultery. This same tension accompanied centuries of romantic literature, even to the middle of the twentieth century, when arranged marriages in the West took a sharp decline.

As one can imagine, romantic love was initially frowned upon. The Church disapproved of adultery and premarital relations, as it continues to do so today. Intrigue at court was far more lenient. Lords and ladies became enthralled by the possibilities, and were less intimidated by ecclesiastical law.

One might expect this to have produced rampant promiscuity, but that never really happened. The taste for romantic love was for intrigue and fantasy more than anything else. People enjoyed listening to tales that entertained and captivated entire courts. Sexual promiscuity would have been dangerous to say the least, but social flirtations gained acceptability. A lord was actually flattered by the courtly attentions that his lady wife received by troubadours, which they made a point of doing at every court they visited. This is how troubadours made a living.

These poems and songs fashioned a literary genre that resulted in voluminous tales of chivalry, adventure and love that we collectively refer to as *Arthurian Literature*. These stories dominated the intellectual landscape for centuries.

A young knight had to prove himself worthy of the lady of his affections. He strove to improve his skills and character and perform great deeds — all this in the name of love. Reputation and honor meant everything.

The tales of Lancelot and Guenevere, Tristan and Isolde, and many others, overflowed with adventures of daring and longing. The knight showed his love as much through fairness and grace as martial skill and bravery. Social expectations grew from there.

Western male ethics were advancing in leaps and bounds.

Principles summarized by the Twelve Trusts gained popular appeal and made significant cultural contributions. What was once a warrior tradition for the elite, became the moral under-current of all Western male ethics.

The freedom exemplified by courtly love drifted beyond great halls of castles and influenced entire societies. Transcending the limits of courtly flirtation and extramarital affairs, it became *romantic*.

***

Romantic love transformed gender relationships almost overnight. Women became a source of inspiration to men and could no longer be considered chattel. Men willingly served them instead. This is why powerful women sponsored writers and troubadours to craft the finer aspects of chivalry. Everyone seemed to benefit. Everyone but the Church, that is, which gradually but steadily lost some of its control over people's lives.

Women were on the ascendancy, along with the value of individual preferences and autonomy. The social upheaval caused by romantic love could not be silenced. Fictional heroes, who culturally reflected the times while influencing change, seemed more real than their antiquated predecessors. Earlier warriors, like Beowulf, were more interested in battle *armor* than *amour*. In contrast, Lancelot and Tristan were celebrated for matters of the heart, introducing a refreshingly idealistic panoply of knights, complete with white horses, shining armor, and unmatched fighting skills. Men were inspired by these new heroes and that pleased women too.

As time went on, romantic love so attached itself to people's hopes and imagination that some of its magic survives even today. Almost every love story we read or watch at the movies takes its shape from those early medieval romances.

***

Romantic love is an idealized interpretation of love between a man and a woman, a state of affection that transcends all other relationships.

While its passion certainly includes sexual attraction, at its core lies a deeper urge for personal fulfillment. When you find true love, the person you need to be with for the rest of your life, little else matters.

It usually starts with a powerful feeling of simpatico. She is not just someone you feel attracted to, or want to join with sexually. You feel irresistibly drawn by what seems an existential need for completion, as if she were once part of you and needs to be reclaimed. Desire is strong, but anxiety is often stronger.

Medieval writers took care in describing this exaggerated process in minute detail. This love starts when the eyes first meet, sending a message of certainty to the heart that cannot be refused without injury or even death. *I cannot live without her; I can only live for her; here is where my life belongs.*

Reality splits into two, the dominant reality of the loved one, and then, in the faded background, everything else. This provokes a whole new paradigm of meaning.

Only by uniting with that other person can this existential

need be met. When such love happens, or even when you *think* it happens, it becomes a powerful, life-transforming experience.

This special woman becomes the focal point of your life from which you cannot easily escape. Your very existence seems to depend on her. If sexual attraction were likened to gravitational pull, the obsession of romantic love becomes a planetary orbit. Here is the center of your universe.

This process is not always a positive experience. It can be a source of terrible anxiety. Falling in love incurs a sudden avalanche of unexpected risks. What if she does not like you? What if she turns away before you express your feelings? What if her parents think you unworthy? She may already be spoken for, or even married. What if you make a fool of yourself? Or someone more worthy pushes you aside? How could you possibly survive?

The tension of what to do and what to avoid results in tongue-twisted foolishness that the medieval audience considered endearing. Lancelot, as an eighteen year old, freshly made knight, went dumb when he first met Guenevere. Unable to speak, he was oblivious to her witty insults. From that moment on, he dedicated his entire life to her.

Did he try to seduce her? No. He committed himself to a quest to prove himself worthy of love, and dedicated every victory to his queen. In fact, to avoid appearing foolish, he did his best to keep away from her. At one point he nearly drowned in her presence, forgetting to control his horse while crossing a stream.

Making himself worthy for Guenevere became his sole reason to live. For years his reputation increased, even as he shielded his name, referring to himself only as the *Queen's Knight*.

It was Guenevere who finally chose to reward her champion with a kiss, which led to their inevitable affair.

Sometime later, while Arthur was with another woman, Lancelot and Guenevere finally consummated their love. Their affair lasted over twenty years, through bouts of jealousies and several turns of events. Lancelot tried to end the affair after he failed to achieve the Holy Grail, but their love was re-ignited. Throughout everything, he remained loyal to King Arthur in every respect but that, and his medieval audience did not condemn him.

Lancelot was often tormented by his longing and the seeming impossibility of fulfillment. From that initial, all-consuming anxiety, to proving himself over and over against all odds, to besmirching his great honor through hidden trysts, to failing in the Grail Quest, and losing his position as Arthur's greatest knight. At one point his suffering led to temporary madness.

Joseph Campbell, author of the *Power of Myth*, pointed out the power of romantic love. In a medieval world that firmly believed in the eternal punishment of hell, Sir Tristan feels compelled, even honor-bound, to accept such a fate rather than deny his love for Queen Isolde. What is significant is that readers did not consider him wrong for doing so. True love was deemed worthy of risking your immortal soul.

Things have changed. Disposable relationships now occupy us until something better comes along. We have premarital contracts to protect us from any loss in making a mistake in our choice of marriage. The question is this: Has something been gained? Or lost?

***

The medieval image of romantic love is greeted warily by modern expectations. We are too cynical to accept its exaggerated claims, much less its dreamy promises. Attractive though it may be, it does not fit the world we live in. Although we want something like the kind of love that medieval writers describe, we conclude that its unrealistic expectations will lead to inevitable disappointment. Romance is for novels and movies, with violins playing in the background. We live in a world of online dating and infidelity. Half of all marriages end in divorce. All around us, relationship after relationship fails. Even the ones that survive do not necessarily look happy as spouses argue or ignore each other, becoming little more than resentful roommates.

Deep in our hearts, in men's as well as women's, we long for the heartfelt dance of love, the whirlwind of emotion that comes from its discovery. Nothing quite compares. We want just the right fit, the comfort of home after a long journey, never to part again. We want this because it provides a validation of life like nothing else can. Something is missing without it, like a happy dream nagging at our memory after we awake.

Do we have the qualities it takes to make such a love possible?

Are we responsible for our own failings? Maybe we are not willing to do what it takes, or are not capable of the endurance and compromise. It is easy to say that romantic love is an illusion for fools, when that is how we look at it.

Distilled from its medieval trappings, romantic love still represents an idealized relationship between a man and woman for us today. As an idealized anything, it is something we aim for, but never fully attain. Unfortunately, it does not fall from heaven, as part of some preordained destiny. Neither can we wish it into existence.

What we can do is work at bringing it into our lives as completely as possible, just like all our chivalric ideals. And chivalry helps us do just that.

Here is what most people fail to realize. Romantic love depends on the same principles, all of them, that are listed in our code. *Fostering these principles in our lives makes such love possible by providing the attributes of character to sustain it.*

The love I describe comes to life in the commitment of two people who are honest, faithful and loyal. It requires fair treatment of one another that comes from a sense of justice, while accepting each other's imperfections. This is the same principle that mercy thrives on. Humility is also required. The boastful heart has no room for love. Honor, respect and courtesy provide everyday substance and expression. Each partner would willingly give his or her life to save the other.

Simply put, when we strive for such love, when we hone our own personalities to make it possible, we increase our chances for a stronger and better relationship than if we do not. No magic here. No sitting around waiting for it to happen, and then blaming our partners when it fails. If we want such a love, we *can* draw it into our grasp. We are reminded of that universal truth, you reap what you sow.

Taking all this into consideration, chivalry insists that there is no greater test of your principles than a close relationship with a woman you love. Either your ideals grow stronger or you prove how superficial they really are. Romantic love demands your best efforts at all times. It directs you to realistically conceive the ideal relationship in your mind, in partnership with the woman you love, and make it happen.

If you achieve this kind of love, it will play an important part in your process of self-development. Why? Because you will develop your skills and personal attributes for someone other than yourself. Chivalry tells us that the love you feel for a loved one should supersede love of self. Here we find the purest instinct of the warrior spirit.

As someone who has known this kind of love after a lifetime of searching, and has been moved by it profoundly, I say without hesitation that it is worth all your efforts.

***

I believe in romantic love.

I also agree with cynics who claim that romantic love exists only in our minds. Is that a contradiction? Where else would love, loyalty, faithfulness, and concern for others exist but in our minds?

Ideals are imaginary perfections that we do not find in our imperfect reality. Nevertheless, unreachable goals point the way to self-improvement, personal fulfillment and a full experience of abundant life. In this respect, Chivalry-Now represents a complete philosophy.

Unlike Eastern philosophies, we do not claim to have perfect masters. Our Western heels are so firmly planted on the ground that we would not know what to do with them. We are beneficiaries of rational thinkers, objective historians, scientists. Most of us would rather be spiritually inquisitive than corralled into some formula of faith. We prefer weighing the facts than automatically saying "I believe." Many of us who claim to be religious usually keep our minds open to new discoveries. We accommodate who we are by purposely separating church from state.

Faith-healing may fascinate us, but we prefer to consult a good physician when we get ill.

This skepticism and independence forms the heart of Western culture at its best. We do not charge blindly forward. We keep our eyes open; we examine alternatives; we listen to different opinions. We don't chant for the deaths of our enemies in the street, or believe that the random killing of innocent people brings an end to violence.

We prefer logical solutions to fanaticism, which is why democracy works well for us. This is who we are. When something does not work, or when it ceases to have value, we place it aside and move on. More traditional societies have trouble doing this.

Mystical claims do not move us so much as realistic possibilities. We may fall victim to nationalism occasionally, but our conscience eventually pulls us back on track. We tolerate those among us who would trade what we have for a theocracy, but strongly resist when they go too far. Hence the surge of books by atheists and agnostics following the evangelical flourishing that took place during the administration of George W. Bush.

We are not perfect, but then again, we never claimed to be.

Idealistic possibility, coupled with realism, has a propensity of transforming cold reality no matter how long it takes. This is where our trust of freedom comes from. Our hope for building a better world based on a given track record.

Like any virtue, romantic love does not exist until we bring it to life within ourselves. That's true of all ideals. What is honor to a man who is not honorable? Defending those in need only happens when we make it happen. Courtesy comes to life when people act courteously. Our code urges us to bring these human constructs to life.

So too, the attainment of romantic love.

***

The man who wants to be loved more than he wants to give love, misses the point entirely. The truest benefit of love is how you are transformed by what you feel.

When you really love someone, it changes your whole perspective of life. Your heart beats faster. The world seems brighter. The future looks more secure. You feel fulfilled and excited at the same time. You are happy. Your priorities change.

Unfortunately, we enter the world wanting people to love us. We vie for attention like baby birds competing in a nest. We are told that we have to love ourselves first, but almost immediately self-love gets in the way of things. The self-focus of self-love is unending because it is not really love. Love is always directed toward someone else. Self-love is a form of ruinous greed that has invaded a realm where it has no place. It is the promise of temporary satisfaction that comes from winning a prize. It cannot produce the experience, dare I say *magic*, of romantic love. From the perspective of romance, your relationship is doomed.

Likewise, romantic love does not measure how your loved one feels toward you. It measures how you feel toward her.

Despite Western society's preoccupation with getting what you want, it is possible to be completely in love with someone who has no feelings for you at all. You can richly benefit from unrequited love. That is because the true beauty of love comes from loving, not from being loved. When both happen, however, the circle is complete.

If you want to experience true love, you have to be open to it first — welcome it when it arrives, and cherish it quietly even when things go wrong. It is the *commitment* to love that brings new life.

***

Men often feel insecure when it comes to matters of love.

Facing the woman you feel attracted to, you may fall silent, restless, and stumble over words like a teenager in the first throes of puberty. Even worse, you may get loud and verbose, or pretend to be more important than you are, boasting and bragging. Nervous in her company, you may try to impress her with a barrage of senseless humor.

Although the woman may smile, most likely she wants to leave. Would you not feel the same?

A secure man does not *try* to impress people. His quiet reassurance and comfortably polite manners say everything that needs to be said.

When courting a woman, the best way to impress her is by throwing away stupid one-liners and contrived strategies. Build a friendship instead. Make her comfortable in your presence. Discover her interests rather than dominating her with yours. Enjoy polite, personable exchanges without trying to push her into the bedroom. If you respect her as a person, she will respect you as well, which is a very good start. If you want to impress her, let chivalry quietly express itself in what you do and say, without being pushy or self-absorbed:

- Smile when you greet her. Make it clear you enjoy her company.
- Be kind, patient, attentive, and always courteous.
- Be honest and faithful.
- Listen with genuine interest. A first date is not an audition, with this woman as your audience.
- A little dignity goes a long way.
- Recognize her value as a person.
- Be protectively strong, but not overbearing.
- Learn who she is, while being who you are.
- A little humor is valuable, but treat it like seasoning — just enough to spice the moment to her liking.

Don't forget the social niceties that chivalry is famous for: opening doors, carrying heavy packages, giving up your seat on a bus, smiling in a friendly manner, waiting for her to eat before you start, walking on the outside of the sidewalk, rising when she enters the room. Show you are polite with other women as well, while still making her feel special. Even if you know right away that the connection is not there, don't gawk at other women, or flirt with the waitress. While this woman is with you, she is your date. Respect her for that.

Be careful not to overdo social niceties. Some women have been so scarred by men that they do not trust any man's intentions, especially behavior that is overly polite. A few might find it uncomfortable or even patronizing. This does not mean discarding your ideals. Quite the opposite. It means responding to her discomfort by toning down your actions. How she feels is more important than putting chivalry on display.

I once knew a wonderful fellow who went to extremes around

a particular young woman. Every time the tip of her cigarette accumulated ash, he would rise from his chair with an ashtray and catch it before it fell. He must have done this half a dozen times during the conversation, making everyone in the room uncomfortable, especially the woman who just wanted to enjoy her smoke. That would be courtesy gone awry.

Some final advice for the seeking bachelor: don't be afraid to smile, with the warmth and confidence of a man of dignity. We see a lot of stony faces on men. Permanent scowls. They try to look angry, like a warning: *stay away; keep out of my space; watch out, I'm trouble.* They think it makes them look manly or important, little knowing how their insecurity shoos people away.

I am not sure if Clint Eastwood invented this harsh, stay-away-from-me demeanor, but he certainly capitalized on it. He taught nearly a whole generation of insecure men how to look disagreeably threatening. I fail to see how this helps anyone. Men who act that way seem two-dimensional. For women who do not know better, it may seem attractive at first, but they soon find out that little else follows.

***

A few words about loyalty to friends.

This is the second half of the eighth Trust, and an integral part of romantic love as well.

In chivalry, friendship is a joining of hearts and minds of people who share part of one another's journey, which is their quest. Their lives and interests intersect in many ways. Coming from different perspectives, thoughts are shared to enhance each other's growth. They come to each other's aid when needed. Even when things go well, they are concerned with one another's well-being.

To have a close friend you can speak with openly, whose

sincerity is unquestioned and whose opinions you value, is like discovering an oasis in the desert. Here you find the kind of respite that refreshes mind and spirit.

Heartfelt communications between friends can be cathartic as well as challenging and informative. We are social creatures who need such closeness and sharing. It should never be perceived as a threat or sign of weakness.

Personal nobility shows itself most readily in friendship. The loyalty it fosters is not blind, but borders more on kinship. Here we find our metaphorical *Round Table,* each friend seated at his or her place. Their strength of hand and heart strengthens our own, just as ours strengthens theirs.

We are multiplied among them — our principles purified and prepared for the challenges that await us. In Chivalry-Now we call such friends Companions.

Chapter 12

"Abhor Scandal and Gossip…"

Trust # 9: I will abhor scandal and gossip — neither partake nor delight in them.

Writing a chapter about scandal and gossip was far more challenging than I expected.

The topic had to be included as one of the Twelve Trusts, but its tenor seemed different from the others — almost mundane by comparison. The others made positive assertions about ideals, while this one formed a prohibition, like an Old Testament *Thou Shalt Not…*

We are told to *abhor* certain behavior rather than delight in it. This suggests that delighting or partaking in someone else's ruin is a common tendency that needs to be avoided. Nothing stops a person in his or her tracks more quickly than a juicy piece of gossip.

As common as this is, the Ninth Trust tells us to *hate* it in no uncertain terms.

Before we accept or reject this principle out-of-hand, we need to examine what it is trying to say. As often happens with Chivalry-Now, the full significance of an ideal lies hidden until we explore its depth.

Abhorring gossip does not mean never talking about someone else, or dismissing a person's misfortune as if it never happened. It does not mean avoiding a sense of satisfaction when a criminal gets fairly punished, or being pleased when hypocrisy is revealed for what it is. It does not mean we must decide against warning some innocent person about a trouble-maker.

The essence of the Ninth Trust has to do with behavior that arises from contempt for other people, an attitude that enjoys someone else's misfortunes, as if frailties and guilt were not something we all share. It is often related to jealousy or envy, and is meant to hurt rather than protect. It tends to fixate on a morbid, vicarious fascination. Like watching a car wreck, you feel pleased that you are not that other person.

Gossip heals nothing. It repairs nothing. It degrades all who partake in it. It breeds self-righteousness that is based on self-deception.

"Let he who is without sin cast the first stone." The person who habitually gossips imitates the role of being sinless, enjoying the license to throw as many stones as possible. Such incredible conceit compounds his evil intent.

From chivalry's standpoint, delighting in gossip and scandal is an affront to humility and to honor. It makes one less of a warrior and more of a scavenger, picking over the bones of some carrion in the field. It is an insult to our gender, and to humanity as a whole.

***

At the end of our lives we learn that reputation is all we ever really owned — a long time in the making, and easily ruined.

The person who gossips feels entitled to contribute to the destruction of someone else's reputation, just to be the center of attention. He adds uncalled-for punishment on top of whatever else has already fallen. The prime energy, however, comes not from the object of gossip so much as the person who disseminates it. Like the ringmaster at a circus, all eyes turn toward him as if he has a strange kind of authoritative capacity. It is a cry for attention gained at someone else's expense.

Gossiping is an unsavory habit that is difficult to break. It becomes part of your personality, a character flaw that degrades the finer aspects of who you are.

While gossiping may gain you episodic popularity, the cost to your character is great. Your moral inhibitor, that part of conscience that regulates behavior, shuts off, giving you not only permission but a veritable mandate to destroy people's lives. Power. This can be so socially addictive that you find yourself thinking of new avenues for gossip every waking hour of the day. Just remember, it is not necessarily you that listeners like, just the voyeurism of gossip. You are probably the last person anyone would trust.

What do you become when this happens? A truth-teller that everyone can depend on for the latest news? A prosecutor, with executioner-like tendencies? An avenging angel who is well known for "saying-it-like-it-is?"

None of these really. What habitual gossip makes you, quite simply, is a reprehensible back-stabbing person who cannot be trusted.

You become a source of suffering to your many victims, just to enhance your own dark feeling of power. Yes, *victims*. You may justify your poison by saying he or she deserved it, but the question then arises: what do *you* deserve? Who assigned you to mete out punishment while delighting in people's ruin? Gossips act more like demons than avenging angels as they profit from the sins of others, instigating what trouble they can. The demon metaphor holds true, for the amount of damage becomes incalculable, rippling out to others in unexpected ways.

Is it any wonder that we include this principle as part of our code?

Gossip becomes a source of power to those who worship it — power to destroy, separate, tear-down, embarrass; power to modify the facts with each retelling; power to appeal to the very worst in human nature and beguile others to do likewise — all the while blaming someone else.

***

In Lord Tennyson's masterpiece *Idylls of the King*, Arthur included the following in his Round Table oath:

Speak no slander, nor listen to it.

In other renditions, he tells his knights *to flee from scandal*, as if it were a devouring beast impossible to destroy.

From these quotes the Ninth Trust finds its Arthurian roots.

If his nephews, Sirs Agrivaine and Mordred, had kept that promise, Arthur's kingdom would have been spared its tragic end, although this was not why Arthur included it. He made it part of the Round Table oath because he knew it would greatly enhance the noble character of his knights, so that their renown would be praised throughout the world.

Arthur understood that habitually delighting in gossip and scandal is a damaging character flaw. One's character is instantly improved by refusing to participate.

Spying and whispering in dark corners is incongruous with manly openness. There is no such thing as innocent gossip. The person who gossips takes someone else's grief and multiplies it through the telling, encircling each person who stays to listen.

Chivalry turns its back on this.

In King Arthur's story, rumors had spread about Sir Lancelot having an affair with the queen. This was not surprising, since many people were involved in assisting with their assignations, including many of Lancelot's kin.

Some suggested that Arthur knew about it all along, but was so busy with his own mistresses that he turned a blind eye.

Sir Agrivaine had long been envious of Lancelot. One day, while drinking heavily, he brooded about how the king was being betrayed by his closest knight. He decided to confront Arthur with the scandal and asked his brothers to join him. Gawain, Gareth and Geharis refused to be part of this and walked away. Sir Mordred, the eldest, agreed to accompany Agrivaine to the king, where they confronted him with their outrage.

Arthur could no longer ignore it. Adultery with the queen was considered treason.

At this point, the noble character of the entire story noticeably crumbles.

Arthur's kingdom had enjoyed peace, mercy and rule of law for over twenty years. The people flourished under the firm yet gentle hand of chivalry. Arthur was considered the ideal king, and Lancelot, despite his shortcomings, the ideal knight. To separate them jeopardized everything.

The lovers were found together. Lancelot escaped, killing most of those who sought to entrap them. The queen was arrested, found guilty, and sentenced to death. Half of the Round Table knights remained loyal to Lancelot — his relatives and friends. With their help, Lancelot and his kin rescued her, killing many of Arthur's knights in the process. Gareth and Geheris, who sided with Lancelot in their hearts, were among those who died.

Arthur followed Lancelot to France and laid siege to his castle. Back in Britain, Mordred convinced the remaining barons to make him king in Arthur's stead. Arthur learned of this and immediately returned. Mordred greeted him with an army, leading to a series of indecisive battles. Hearing what happened, Lancelot quickly returned to fight at Arthur's side, but was too late. The king was dead, along with Mordred and almost all of Arthur's knights.

The destruction of Arthur's world was instigated by pride, envy, ambition — *and gossip*. All that remains is the legend.

***

In my Chivalry-Now emails, I often close with words that encapsulates our core principles: *Truth and Honor*.

These words provide a simple rule to judge our everyday

decisions.

Is it true? Is it honorable? The answer to each of these questions needs to be yes.

While gossip may or may not be true when spoken, it is never honorable.

What honor comes from delighting in the misfortune of another human being, who is just as fallible as the rest of us? Or by fueling outrage over the same? The image it conjures is not heroic or manly. The image is small, spiteful, morally corrupt, a destroyer of people's lives, taking joy from their sorrows and disappointments.

The person who habitually gossips can be likened to a thief or murderer, whose conscience is so distorted that evil is justified by envy, baseless dislike, or even habit.

I knew a woman who smugly referred to this as *fun and games*. Many think common gossip is harmless entertainment, even a social necessity, akin to small talk. But is it? How would you feel if you were the target?

Should the Golden Rule not apply?

Chivalry tells us to constantly rise above frivolous behavior that borders on maliciousness. The very dynamic drains our moral standing. Honor cannot be so diluted as to accommodate the lust for gossip.

***

Lao Tzu, the Taoist sage who wrote the *Tao Te Ching*, said that we should treat victory in battle like a funeral, because men have died.

Here we find the deeper meaning of the Ninth Trust. Human failings, such as crime and war and scandal, are tragic. They should not be the focus of gossipy delight. Whenever an innocent child grows up to be a criminal or rapist or unethical businessperson, it is something to be mourned. When we fail to see the human loss of their misguided lives, not just that of their victims, we slice away a portion of humanity from our concern, and that is reason for shame.

I am not saying that we should coddle criminals, or give them excuses for their behavior, or not hold them to strict requirements of justice.

What I mean is simply this: any brother who falls is a cause for sorrow, not derision. As a man, he was meant for better things.

During times of war, we tend to objectify the enemy. This may be necessary on the battlefield for the soldier to accomplish his duty, but at some point we have to recognize that the enemy is made up of people, often innocent people. Perhaps war could be better avoided if we start from that simple conclusion.

Gossip can be avoided as well, especially if we look behind its attractive façade and see the suffering it causes.

All this comes down to seeing the results of what we do. The trouble is, the attention that comes from sharing gossip, the feeling of power it gives us, blinds us to the pain we cause. Now, some people might say that they just do not care. The attention and sense of power is all they care about. Suffice it to say, such a completely selfish attitude runs contrary to the requirements of chivalry.

So, how do we change this if gossip is already a strong personal weakness?

It will not be easy. The lure can be very powerful — so much so that I can think of only one way to resist it — *with loathing*.

The Trust tells us exactly that.

To *abhor* means to detest, to regard with loathing. These words are so negatively charged they almost seem to come from somewhere else. The distinction between East and West shows itself most distinctly here. We are not told to view all things with an equal lack of passion. When something is wrong, we recognize it as such, and resist its power. To do this, we have to see it for what it is, and for the suffering it causes.

In Western philosophy, life is not an illusion — although we often fill it with illusions, and delude ourselves with false ideas. We are charged to resist evil, not to accept that this is just the way things are. This grasp of reality and respect for truth is where the disciplines of science came from. We do not know everything, but we are determined to know more.

Some may say that our thirst for understanding and changing the world we live in is as much of a curse as it is a blessing. On one hand we have vaccines to eliminate diseases, and agricultural techniques that can feed the world. On the other, we have weapons of mass destruction, environmental pollution, and people still starve.

This is where morality needs to assert itself.

Conscience tells us to speak out and defend what is right. Exceptionally brave individuals go so far as to risk their lives to protect the innocent. But first we need to apply some thought into our actions. Intelligence and self-control are paramount.

When it comes to gossip and scandal, there are times when we must confront people in the name of truth and compassion. Most often, our meaning can be made by walking away with dignity and honor, refusing to partake in hateful discourse. When confronted by it on television or radio, we can shut it off.

***

The ideals of chivalry always seem greater than our capacity to realize them. Ideals represent a perfection that human beings just are not capable of. They stand as goals for us to strive for in order to improve ourselves and experience a level of authenticity we might otherwise miss. While chivalry expects our very best efforts, it realistically assumes that mistakes will be made. It calls us toward perfection, but never expects us to reach it. That would be impossible. Whenever we fail, chivalry tells us to learn from our failure and try again.

From this perspective, we know that it is wrong to judge an entire person solely by his or her mistakes. We are the totality of our lives, the sum of our every thought, word and deed. As we try to improve, what matters most is that the good significantly outweighs the bad. Chivalry recognizes and honors our best attributes such as they are, while always encouraging us to do better.

When we respond to gossip and slander, we deny our brother or sister this bit of human redemption that chivalry makes so plain. Their faults and frailties put them on the outside, so we can assail them with pot-shots whenever we please. We deny them redemption by inferring that their weaknesses make them worse than us.

It may be true. They may be worse than us. But that can change. By stitching someone's vest with a scarlet letter, are we not heaping shame upon shame, making reconciliation that much more difficult?

It is easy to fuel anger and jealousy, or dwell on some offense until our sense of justice screams for satisfaction. These are all very real emotions. Nevertheless, trading gossip is the lowest form of approaching justice — and lessens who we are at the same time.

***

The fellow who habitually gossips does not walk away unscathed. The act eventually shapes and defines him in ways he never expected, like an addiction designed to propagate itself. Gossip becomes a vital component of his socializing with others, often his first choice of discourse, even with strangers. He assumes that everyone shares his enthusiasm for *dirt*.

His inner goodness contends with mixed priorities. You might see him doing volunteer work for a nonprofit event, whispering about others who attend it. He pigeonholes every person that he meets for future reference, identifying this one for a mistake that happened 20 years ago, and another for her taste in clothes. If the one over there ever got caught committing a crime, nothing else needs to be remembered.

Amateur and professional gossips love the mistakes and sorrows of other people, and that in itself subverts who they are. They might not see how they engage in emotional thievery and even the murder of people's reputations. This is the scandal that they instigate and participate in, but fail to recognize. Chances are that they would not like people like themselves.

An insurmountable chasm separates the person who lives for gossip from the advocate of chivalry. They are opposites. One cherishes dark corners and unsavory opportunism, while the other values truth, second chances and personal honor. You cannot carry them both.

***

The knight-errant is known for his word. He acquires trust from others because he earns their trust.

That means speaking with the kind of integrity befitting a man of honor. His reputation is forged on honesty and reflects a profound lack of maliciousness. He is one of those rare people you can safely open your heart to, because his values are reliable, like a rock.

Cheap gossip does not fit in. When gossip is directed his way, he leaves or smiles with polite disappointment and declines to comment.

His words are chosen with care. If you listen carefully, you hear a depth of understanding you will not hear elsewhere, because his vision of the world is part of everything he says and does. He is an anchor of stability in a world rushing madly toward oblivion.

His words slice to the core of whatever matter he speaks of like a fine edged sword — thoughtful, never wasted, powered by insight, honesty and patience.

The true knight is charged to serve as a conduit of truth in a world fraught with illusion and discontent. That is his task more than any other.

Lies, gossip and conspiracies are anathema to everything the knight stands for. They are darkness to his light, smoke to his transparency.

If knighthood is your goal, take care of what you say and do. Examine how you really feel, and how that feeling affects your judgment. Introduce your passions to your peace loving center, and let them know congress.

In the end, the Ninth Trust is about more than gossip and slander. It is about the mindset that revels in them, the vision of self and others that fails to appreciate the tragedy of each person's setback, failure or sin, the smug self-righteousness of the small mind surrendering to evil intent. Chivalry has no tolerance for that.

***

Gossip and scandal are taken to unprecedented extremes by the news media. Here we find the principles of chivalry completely discarded in order to capitalize on human weakness. This is not done by accident, or with closed eyes. The decisions to promote gossipy, salacious, and voyeuristic interests in the population are being made at the highest levels. Commercial news reflects the moral integrity of the tobacco industry, profiting from the destruction of our people.

Their intent is to propagate mass addiction to tawdry scandal. They go so far as to create hardly newsworthy celebrities like Paris Hilton or Anna Nicole Smith, stalk them like hungry wolf-packs, and then viciously attack when they do wrong.

Unfortunately, this has proved an effectively cruel, self-serving formula for selling magazines and boosting viewership. In one way, this astounds me. I know nobody who seems remotely interested in their gossipy chatter, and most people seem notably annoyed. Are they missing the larger audience by not presenting something more respectable?

Listen to the theme music of news shows, generating the excitement they promise to deliver — excitement based on voyeuristic tragedy. Listen to the voices of news anchors or commentators, unashamedly reflecting the tantalizing lure of gossip. Notice the formulaic angles of attack used during interviews, innocent quotes taken out of context, misleading suggestions, embarrassing extremist "consultants" screaming at each other, emulating scandalous behavior of their own. Even political topics reek of titillating gossip.

I sometimes think of them as circus venders trying to attract people to the "Freak Show" that they created and for which they are responsible.

Their audacity is such that they promote themselves by focusing on salacious murders for months at a time, ignoring events that are really newsworthy.

All this comes with a price: a loss of human dignity and respect for truth.

The noble King Arthur was right in telling his famous knights, heroes all, to speak no slander, nor listen to it. This distinguishes a man of honor as much as any virtue, and perhaps more than most.

Chapter 13

"I will be Generous…"

Trust # 10: I will be generous to the poor and to those who need help.

Noblesse oblige is a French term that means *nobility is an obligation.*

In medieval times, it was expected for members of the aristocracy to behave in a manner commensurate to their station. Great power brings great responsibility.

This sentiment was expected of the warrior knight as well. Distinguished from commoners by training, duty and financial support, he was expected to act with honor and benevolence. The interdependency of feudal society depended on this. The common people provided food and taxes that supported the aristocracy and knights of all levels. In return, they were given protection, law and justice.

Largesse, another French term, was part of this obligation. Largesse referred to the kind of liberal generosity that only someone of nobility could afford during medieval times. It was sometimes given as a reward, or to help someone in need, but it could also be given spontaneously, part of the give-and-take of feudalism.

In this way, a generous lord or knight brought energy and loyalty to his people. Today we might view such actions as buying off the poor in order to quell thoughts of rebellion, but this reduces largesse to twenty-first century skepticism. Back then, rewarding good people was considered a normal part of the social milieu, reflecting the beneficence of God as they under-stood it. As much as possible, the aristocracy was expected to represent God's secular will on earth, as the priesthood represented religious obligations. Royalty and clergy were to act in partnership for the good of God's people. Whenever this obligation faltered, tyranny quickly replaced it.

In order to unveil some of the finer points of largesse, I present quotes from a collection of Arthurian stories known as the *Prose Lancelot*. (Quotes taken from *Lancelot of the Lake*, Oxford University Press 1989, translated by Corin Corley.) This massive collection served as the source material for Mallory's *Le Morte d'Arthur*.

I chose the first brief quote to impress the reader with the moral and political insight of the era which we often fail to recognize today.

Its Age of Enlightenment undertones might have enjoyed fellowship with the likes of John Adams, Thomas Jefferson and Benjamin Franklin. Here we find seeds of thought that would later germinate into Western democracy:

> "...the kingdom cannot be held without the consent of the common people."

These words were spoken to King Arthur by someone known as the *worthy man*. This prophetic persona served as a literary device, introducing a voice of conscience and redemption just when the story needed it.

To appreciate the entire message of the worthy man, let us examine the context in which it was given.

King Arthur faces his greatest adversary in the person of Prince Galehaut, a virtuous lord of great renown. Galehaut has already conquered a number of realms with messianic fervor, building an army far larger than Arthur's. His qualities are such that he has also won the love and loyalty of his conquered subjects, who are convinced that Galehaut should be the High King in Arthur's stead.

Arthur, on the other hand, finds his own subjects failing him at every turn.

When the two armies confront each other, Galehaut looks at Arthur's in dismay. Deciding that winning such a disproportionate battle would bring him no honor, he grants Arthur a year's reprieve to build up his army, and then meet for a final contest.

Arthur turns to the *worthy man* for advice, and is castigated for his failings.

Up until this point the reader is led to believe that Arthur was an honorable man, worthy of his title as High King. The worthy man insists otherwise. Finding himself standing at the edge of an abyss ready to fall in, Arthur listens to the man's criticisms, hoping to find a way to rectify things. Using harsh words, the worthy man expounds political realities that are as meaningful today as they were back then:

> "For the right of the poor and the powerless cannot reach you: *instead the faithless rich man is heard and honored before you because of his wealth, while the righteous poor man finds no justice because of his poverty.* The right of widows and orphans has perished under your dominion. God will call you most cruelly to account for this, for He Himself said through the mouth of His prophet David that He is guardian of the poor and sustains the orphans and will destroy sinners. *That is how you take care for God's people*, over whom He has given you dominion. And that will bring you to destruction, for God will destroy the sinners. Therefore He will destroy you..."
> [italics mine]

What he is telling Arthur is that the charge of leadership is to care for the well-being of all citizens, not just the wealthy and powerful. In fact, leaders are required to give the poor special attention in order to ease their burdens and elevate their lot.

Unfortunately, Arthur erred in a way that is common to most

people in power. They cater to the wealthy and powerful, usually at the expense of everyone else.

We see this failure conspicuously in the United States, where corporations usurp power from the people despite the many safeguards of our democratic system. People suffer; the environment is poisoned; war is waged for wrong purposes; our national reputation disintegrates around the world. Only after a constant chain of disasters are we learning that military might is not everything. We have also learned that claiming God's favor does not mean having it. Stubborn pride is too inflexible to reach higher goals. Lying to the people brings only shame and destruction.

We see conservatives blatantly ignoring the needs of our poorer citizens, while liberals make a cottage industry out of disrespectful entitlements. Both are guilty of turning their backs on the heart of a thoughtful patriotism. Both contribute to the poisoning of our culture to the detriment of everyone but special interests. They are blind guides, all of them, for in the end, even special interests share the same world as everyone else, even as they work tirelessly to decimate it. When the symbiotic inter-dependency of life is replaced by a competitive drive for acqui-sition, everyone is eventually brought down.

We should not talk about patriotism at all, or claim to love our country, if we do not love and care for our fellow citizens, *all of them*, the poor, infirmed and uneducated as well. Patriotic words that honor past wars and rich opportunities, while neglecting *our own people*, are false in the eyes of chivalry, cheapening all the values of male ethics.

In the name of *Mammon*, money, we are destroying our capacity to love and care for others and defend those in need — the very qualities that make us men.

This is why we no longer find joy in our lives. When we shut people out in order to find narcissistic treasures, we ignore the basic needs of our brothers and sisters worldwide. What joy do we deserve in a world where over a billion people live in abject poverty? Our collective conscience holds us back. That is why we turn to distractions and alcohol and drugs — to escape our nagging sense of right and wrong.

The answer is easy to find. It stares us gauntly in the face, crying for attention with every hungry child's scream. And yet we ignore it, drowning in the greed that is pushed upon us by those who are greedier still.

The *Prose Lancelot* spells it out in political terms that are relevant today:

> "…do not aim to give them [wealthy people] rich gifts, so much as beautiful and attractive ones, for one should not give a rich man valuable things… for it is a tiresome thing to pile riches upon riches. To the poor man, though, one should give things that have more value than beauty, which are more useful than attractive, for poverty needs only betterment, and riches need only pleasure. The same things should not be given to everyone, for one should not give a man something of which he has plenty."

Interesting advice. Give wealthy people things that are pleasurable, and poor people things that have value, that benefit their lives and raise them to a higher level. It dares to say the obvious: that the rich and powerful are already privileged and have little need. Adding to their riches is not only wasteful, it undermines a delicate social balance by widening the inequity between rich and poor, the haves and have-nots.

By neglecting those in need, Arthur's leadership failed its prime responsibility.

Noblesse oblige requires us to help the poor.

What do we do instead? The very opposite.

We opiate the masses with television and entertainment, what we today consider *pleasurable* diversions, and hand things of great *value* over to the rich, who have no need for them. How does the life of a billionaire directly benefit from tax cuts to the wealthy? What important difference could another billion dollars possibly make in his personal life?

That same money could significantly improve the living conditions of countless poor people, and save the lives of those dying from starvation.

Chivalry-Now requires that we take a stand on this, just as the worthy man tells King Arthur how to change his ways.

The interdependency of human life is strong and complex. We all need each other in order to thrive.

The worthy man, the personification of male conscience, reinforces this plainly:

"…no one was ever destroyed by largesse, but many have been ruined by avarice. Always give plenty and you will have plenty to give."

"…you will never wear out the gold and silver of your land: rather, they will wear you out as the water wears out the millwheel."

The worthy man advises King Arthur how to save both his soul and his realm. He teaches him not just to give to others, rich and poor, but how to give *effectively*. Charity by itself has no meaning. There is a better way.

"…I shall teach you how to heal a sick heart in a healthy body…"

"…humility is a virtue by which one increases and promotes one's honor and advantage."

The generosity of largesse is comprised not only of giving, but also in how you *treat* people generously. It represents the give and take of life, divinely inspired to the religious, inspired by conscience to others. By elevating people's lives, by improving their stations, tearing down barriers and providing them with hope, a greater patriotism arises, a patriotism based not on pride, but on partnership — a whole new vision.

***

The worthy man, who speaks to us all when we listen to our hearts carefully, offers a medieval example of the kind of generosity he means.

He tells Arthur that he should go to every city in his kingdom, and choose a poor but honorable man. He should then leave the company of his barons and magistrates to speak with that man and foster fellowship. Finding the man truly honorable, he should then reward him with a horse.

He tells Arthur not to just give the man a horse, like a Christmas present. He tells him to ride the horse alongside the man to show how much the king values that horse, and then have him ride it. Only then should he transfer ownership, making it a high honor between friends.

It is the human, brotherly touch, illustrated here, that makes generosity special, completely unlike a welfare dole that bears a social stigma while fostering dependence and resentment. Person-to-person, man-to-man — not taxes-to-agency-to-post-office-to-impersonal-mailbox. This is where liberal programs go severely in the wrong direction.

Arthur is told to give in such a way as to honor people's spirits and build self-esteem, so helping them to improve themselves. He can perform this only through genuine humility and concern, not as a gesture to buy votes, or to keep the under-class quiet. By giving a gift synonymous with honor, he seeks to raise their station, which does justice to their humanity while increasing their loyalty and value to the realm.

Arthur is even told to give the poor man money, so that he too can perform largesse toward others, like social ripples in a cultural pond.

Is it wise, however, to leave the company of the rich and powerful to "make much" of a poor man? Would not the barons and magistrates be insulted or think less of him?

The worthy man tells Arthur not to worry.

"The blame of the foolish dies away, and the praise of the wise grows greater and stronger."

How unlike the short-sightedness of politics today.

*****

A true leader should be a man of the people, *all the people* — and that goes right to the heart of knight-errantry as well.

It would be wrong to suggest that historical chivalry ever succeeded in achieving the worthy man's goals. Medieval chivalry constantly suffered from elitism, recognizing only those of the aristocracy or warrior caste. This promoted oppressive arrogance toward people of the lower class, which continued through the Victorian Age, and is still felt today.

The *Prose Lancelot* challenges this concept in no uncertain terms. Even the famous King Arthur had to be humbled by this voice of conscience before he could truly become the ideal king. Arthur wisely did as he was told to secure his kingdom.

A year later, on the eve of battle, Prince Galehaut visited Arthur to perform unexpected homage, becoming the king's loyal friend and ally.

*****

Philanthropy is a wonderful quality for the wealthy to adopt, but the generosity we are discussing is not defined solely by the act of giving. It is a quality of heart and mind that recognizes each person's humanity and responds appropriately. It is a spiritual principle that comes from our vision of the world.

We can define the *poor* as anyone in need. When we listen to a troubled co-worker and offer sound advice, we perform our obligation. Treating people courteously also falls in this domain.

The Tenth Trust should never be viewed as a negative commandment. Giving to charities, volunteering for good causes, donating where needed, are all generous acts that bring fulfillment to the giver as well. They show us another path to personal growth.

Keep in mind, however, that misdirected giving can cause more damage than good. Creating dependency when none is needed is one such example. Others include giving reluctantly or in a demeaning fashion, or with strings attached, or to elicit praise from others, or to gain eternal rewards.

As someone who used to work for the welfare system, I confidently believe that such assistance programs, while performing valuable service, inadvertently demean people they are supposed to help while encouraging dependency. In effect, they sustain people in deplorable situations rather than helping them move on to something better.

I recognize that it is easy to criticize. Finding meaningful solutions at this stage will certainly prove difficult, if not impossible. The problems are too complex, magnified by such factors as lack of education, substance abuse, bad role models, lack of hope and opportunity, discrimination, disabilities, inadequate skills, broken families, negative environments, self-esteem issues — the list never ends. How do we build a program that impacts all these factors according to basic psychological needs?

I do not have the answer, but I do know the direction it needs to take. It needs to be cultural. It needs to connect with people's hearts and inspire what is best in all of us. It means helping people avoid the pitfalls by providing a better path.

If we concentrate on the haves and have-nots, we inadvertently feed into this dichotomy. If we insist that money and success *make the man*, we support a set of values that detracts from us all. If the economy is everything, where does morality fit in? If jobs are more important than protecting the environment, where will people work when the world no longer sustains us? If we believe that the poor cannot help themselves, that is exactly the helplessness we teach them. People tend to rise to their expectations. The purpose of culture is to encourage those expectations, and this is where we fail.

Chivalry-Now is an attempt to remedy our culture so that cooperative answers can be found. It will, in the words of the worthy man, "heal a sick heart in a healthy body."

Here we find our starting point by breaking the circular reasoning that traps us in spiritual stagnation. We are not trapped by what others make us. We are what we make ourselves, with all the possibilities and adventures that come along with that.

In the spirit of Chivalry-Now, largesse means giving of yourself generously to life in all its aspects, but especially to those in need, those whom you are able to seriously help.

Unfortunately, our cultural pride is too weak to do what is necessary to remedy this situation, despite our national wealth and patriotism and religious followings. It is my hope that Chivalry-Now inspires talented people to develop the systematic answers that we need.

***

The Holy Grail is a symbol of grand generosity, a divine cornucopia delivering spiritual and physical nourishment worthy of the quest. It restores the sick to health, the deprived to well-being, and those who are suffering to peace.

When our world suffers and leaders become corrupt, when

men lose their way and things look most hopeless, the Grail appears to us unexpectedly, bringing us the hope and inspiration that we need.

I am not talking about a chalice or jewel that fills the room with light. Those are just symbols. The Grail I speak of is the spark of goodness that expresses itself through conscience, provoking a desire for something better, clarity of sight, and hopefully action.

We perform our Grail requirements through generosity and good works. The *Silent Knight* program is a fine example of this, where knights and dames help people anonymously through designated squires.

Orders of knighthood, such as the *Knights of Columbus*, are famous for humbly performing good deeds. Such formalized groups help the world, but we can all do our part whenever opportunity presents itself, or respond proactively for a worthy cause.

The Grail, as a nourishing vessel, is sometimes referred to as the *eternal feminine*, that which gives of itself abundantly to sustain all life.

While this connotation is amply justified, the Grail can be seen as the *eternal male* as well, a father image leading us toward spiritual victory. It represents what is missing in our psyches that needs to be reclaimed: compassion, hope, generosity, the willingness to sacrifice and take risks.

Our gentler aspects are as masculine as the rest of us, but we tend to identify them with women, who often express these qualities better than we do. This is because we have lost sight of our total nature as men. We resist compassion, thinking it unmanly. In truth, it is a much neglected ingredient of what it means to be a man.

The spirit of generosity reflects the completeness of a man's nature. Its energy fixes things. It repairs people's lives. It lifts the downtrodden, and replaces their pain with dignity. It clears the path for others. It safeguards and protects. It recognizes the likes of Ebenezer Scrooge as someone wounded, a broken man who is no longer functional.

Our search for the Grail is our search for completeness. Giving of ourselves is part of that.

***

Chivalry-Now has no respect for political extremism. Both liberal and conservative philosophies repeatedly fail us in their inflexibility, yet we seem unable to free ourselves from their grip. Their visions are too short-sighted, locked in a contentiously unbending "either/or" approach. Instead of seeing problems for what they are and seeking reasonable solutions, they apply their own philosophies and bend them into a container that will just not fit.

It is insane to think that our moral decisions should be based on taxes, small or large government, or focusing solely on the needs of either the privileged or impoverished.

In a newscast, former Senator Tom Delay forthrightly stated that the two extremes were at war with one another. He made it clear that he meant that quite literally, which explains the terrible win-at-all-costs politics of recent years, that has no regard for virtue or for truth.

Are there only two alternatives to choose from? Would it not be better to place both philosophies aside and see things as they are, without the senseless competition?

What we need is free moral thought, not led by some leader or preacher or guru, but originating in ourselves. We need to free ourselves from the endless, ridiculous swing and counter-swing of pendulum politics and look at our Western nations and the world with new eyes.

***

One final mention.

Generosity, as a virtue, sometimes requires purposeful restraint — that is, *not giving*, in order to quell a particular problem and make independence possible. Parents sometimes need to do this with their children. Tough love.

The underlying virtue of generosity begins with discerning actual need before bestowing anything. Showering a person with gifts, money or attention is not necessarily good. A drug addict may desperately convince you of his need for another fix, just as a spoiled child, who desperately needs discipline, screams for another toy. The thoughtful person who wants to help either the addict or the child knows that acquiescing is not the answer.

Likewise, businesses scream for more privileges in a "free society," striving to find ways to make more money. When their addiction to profit takes control of their moral judgment, they lobby for expanding global markets in ways that hurt other people. They insist on open borders and let others foot the bill. They export jobs overseas at a rate that cripples the working class, while economic indicators mislead us by showing record wealth. Money dependent politicians who forget their obligations cater to those interests while posing to be "a man or woman of the people." Jobs are lost and lives are thrown into despair.

The welfare system provides what they call a *safety net*. Safety from who? From what? Very often from the inconsiderate, immoral actions of the powerful, who hide behind "corporate responsibility."

Generosity needs to be enlightened and far-sighted in its efforts — helping people but always with an eye for the greater good.

The accomplished man of chivalry takes time to learn how best to help others, as well as acting spontaneously. While valuing the individual, he keeps a cautious eye on social and environmental impacts. He gives what he can, but not recklessly.

He seeks to foster hope, confidence and genuine human pride in those he helps, without looking for attention or reward. In other words, he does not give foolishly. He wants what is good, not necessarily what is expedient.

Is it right to help someone while depriving him of what he really needs to learn? Sometimes yes; sometimes no. The mature person has to figure that out.

The doting parent is right to protect his child from harm that a child cannot understand. His efforts do more harm than good if he then neglects teaching his child to become a strong, capable person.

Incautious giving is the shadow side of generosity, where virtue becomes lost in short-sighted action.

Our failure to give wisely in the past has created an under-class of people who have been dependent on welfare for genera-tions. While this reflects the shadow-side of giving on a grand scale, abruptly ending assistance programs, as some want to do, is not the answer. We created this dependency. We are obligated to rectify it without further harming or depriving its victims.

One thing is certain. The answer cannot be found in the close-minded, knee-jerk reactions of either political extreme. We must free ourselves from that perennial mistake.

While the social problems we face in the West are tremendous, the man of chivalry has reason to be optimistic.

History shows us that sometimes it takes a long time for reason and compassion to do what is right...

...but we eventually get around to doing it.

Chapter 14

"I will Forgive..."

Trust # 11: I will forgive when asked, that my own mistakes will be forgiven.

The path toward chivalry can be difficult at times, especially in a world that scarcely recognizes its value.

Many of the roadblocks we face, however, are inside us, cultivated by a lifetime of constant propaganda. One of the most debilitating of these roadblocks is that of *resentment*.

Harboring anger for some offense, day after day, year after year, is a constant drain of spiritual energy that could otherwise be used for personal development. Anger can be so obsessive, even subconsciously, that it ruins our every effort to be free.

It is natural to rebel against injustice, or unfairness, or undeserved insult. Anger is how we respond to wrongdoing. This is true even within the family, where expectations are high and familiarity often breeds contempt.

Such resentment steals the joy from life. The more you try to forget it, the more ingrained it becomes. Over and over the offense plays in your mind of its own accord, screaming for resolution or revenge.

Such anger perverts every virtuous thought with bitter twists and turns and negative attachments. When asked to be generous to the poor, or defend the weak, or be completely just in our actions, we find excuses to say no. "They don't deserve my help. So what if they are treated unfairly. Nobody helps *me*."

In such lifeless soil, the seed of chivalry cannot take hold, and dies.

Anger is one of the strongest, most distracting, self-perpetuating emotions that there is. Like fear, it is also one of the most irrational and destructive. Ego thrives on its intensity, pushing one's true self out of the picture.

How do we conquer such deep-seated resentment? The answer is simple yet difficult to accomplish: by letting it go. By *forgiving* those who offended you so you can move forward. Forgiveness provides a healing and transformational dynamic that leads to personal liberation.

Our culture is so disconnected from its vital roots, however, that it prefers to embrace the dysfunctional rather than embracing a void. For this reason it has ennobled the image of the angry male, from characters portrayed in Clint Eastwood movies, to the in-your-face, war dance mimicry of rap music.

We have been taught to associate habitual anger with power and masculinity rather than seeing it for what it is, the inability to deal with life's problems effectively. We feel its energy and sense its appropriateness. When things go wrong, we have a right to be angry. But why do we take this path so easily? Because the birthright of our identity, our cultural definition of manhood, has been denied us — a deprivation that affects us every minute of the day.

Will anger bring our inheritance back? Will it contribute anything to reconstructing who we are for the better? Or will it aggravate our problems even more?

While anger sometimes has its place, and is capable of providing intense motivation, it cannot restore our original nature, the nobility of man that needs to be recognized and nourished. We need to let it go.

***

Peace can be found in forgiving others.

Unfortunately, our rush and tumble world discourages reconciliation. It prefers contention and rage and endless, uncompromising complaints.

This is where we have failed as men. We have failed to build a saner, better, safer world for ourselves and our families. We failed miserably and we keep on failing, as if failure itself were the unspoken goal — which it is to those who are cynical or otherwise profit from it. How is it that there are men who prefer counterproductive martyrdom to peace? Bloodshed to co-operation? Why do some men scorn the defenseless rather than rushing to their aid? How is it possible that some even kill for reasons of pride, or abuse women in order to feel strong? Such responses are contrary to the basic principles of manhood, and yet society is plagued by them.

There are less dramatic examples of small-minded men who honor justice and truth only when convenient, who smile when they cheat and get away with it.

We might respond with loathing for such men, but chivalry chides us not to. We are asked to work with them instead, with the aim of opening their eyes to something better. How else can we build a world of compassion and forgiveness? Reconciliation is an open door. This does not mean turning our backs on justice, or allowing thieves and liars to take advantage of us. It means having a mind that is open enough to help our brothers extricate themselves from cultural insanity.

We are here to help when possible. Anything less is not chivalry.

***

Sometimes that debilitating feeling we carry cannot be cured by forgiving others for past offenses. It can only be cured by *forgiving ourselves.*

What is more devastating than self-resentment? If you dislike yourself, can you honestly feel worthy enough to improve yourself as well? Can you properly help others when your whole perspective begins from a dark corner of bitterness?

In medieval times, sinners made distant pilgrimages on their knees hoping to earn forgiveness. Today, people turn to psychotherapy, or surrender their autonomy to spiritual leaders or ancient revelation, hoping to find inner peace. Unfortunately, by reaching for self-forgiveness through others, they turn their backs on the only remedy possible.

Whenever we act in a way that offends our core principles, we offend ourselves at the deepest level, for that is where our principles originate — as expressions of ourselves. We split into two conflicting parts, the offender and the offended. This detracts from our spiritual integrity.

This diversion is only real because we make it real. We give it life through our own participation, thereby losing sight of who we are.

Can "self-forgiveness" repair the damage? It cannot — for there is no such thing.

We heal nothing by continuing the charade of self-division that such forgiveness implies, one half trying to forgive the other. There is only a single person. We can no more forgive ourselves than we can love ourselves — another maxim that makes no sense. When we try, we further the delusion of separateness and ego, and make things worse. Wrestle as we may during the dark night of the soul, we wrestle with an angel who is not there. We wrestle with ego, which is nothing more than a self-perpetuated illusion.

Forgiving ourselves is really a metaphor for *personal reconciliation*. We can only achieve this by rejecting the duality we created in our psyche, and seeing ourselves as completely whole.

In our Judeo-Christian tradition, the bible stresses the importance that God is *One*. "Hear ye, oh Israel, the Lord thy God, the Lord is One."

This is very different from saying that there is only one God. In fact, the statement is meaningless unless the singularity of God was previously confused with being a plurality. It highlights the unity of consciousness, in whose image, the Bible claims, we are made. Spirituality is composed of the unity of disparate parts, forming a new singularity greater than its sum. It is that unity that defines us.

The gospels use forgiveness not as an end, but as a stepping stone to something greater: personal redemption.

"Your sins are forgiven. *Go and sin no more.*" (Words spoken by Jesus to an adulteress, after dispelling those who would have her stoned.)

"A man must be *born again*, Nicodemus..." (Jesus explaining how to attain the Kingdom of God to a learned Pharisee.)

Both of these statements speak of change, transformation, the ending of one life for the resurgence of another. In the first quote, forgiveness leads to the primary mandate of "sin no more," which connotes personal change. The second quote ignores forgiveness entirely and gets right to the point: our spiritual life begins with a new birth, a new identity, a new way of seeing things.

Self-forgiveness is an easy catchphrase, but it is totally meaningless. The new life we need is a fundamental grasp of authenticity.

In line with Christian symbolism, it means taking up one's cross, one's moral responsibilities, and moving forward with a new clarity of vision. It means letting go of one's social and even familial inheritance in order to find deeper inspiration.

We only dissolve our guilt and self-resentment when we move forward as a single, complete, authentic person. This liberation occurs when we live more consciously in the moment.

There are times in our lives when we act contrary to our deepest principles. We may hurt someone we love. We may cheat, or steal. We might support wrong causes for personal gain. We may gossip or delight in scandal, or degrade women, or fail to respond to those in need. The more we do these things, the further we drift from our truest nature. When our culture fails to encourage a better path, preferring to feed upon our weaknesses, what results can there be other than discontent and confusion? We may want to forgive ourselves and start anew, but we do not know how. We turn to this preacher or that guru, who manages to distract us for a while, but our original problems remain intact.

Our propensity to err is human. Our inability to easily correct ourselves is human as well. This is where culture is supposed to help. When it does not, we have to take the necessary steps ourselves.

***

Before my knighting ceremony, I was somewhat reluctant about accepting the accolade. It was a serious, life-changing commitment, and something inside me preferred to leave the door open for alternatives. That way, if I ever wanted to stray from my own ideals, I could do so with a clear conscience. I wanted to hold onto the past, despite whatever guilt that entailed, because that was my identity. As a child of this broken culture, did I really want a life based on principles that society no longer respected?

What finally convinced me was a simple question: What is the alternative?

I ask you that now: What is the alternative? The same dull pain and disappointments as before? A constant stream of meaningless distractions? Reaching out for Round Table consciousness with one hand, while holding onto the Wasteland with the other?

For me, I wanted the integrity of rejecting, once and for all, the living-death of an ego-centric, consumer mentality. I preferred the directives of my own chosen ideals rather than past sins, or someone else's coercion.

I admire those of my Companions who come to Chivalry-Now

without having to conquer major dragons of uncertainty. The values they voice so clearly, right from the start, are truly inspirational. I am humbled and strengthened by their vision.

***

The Chivalry-Now explorer becomes a knight-errant when he frees himself from the past and commits himself to the future. That means freeing himself from any false perceptions and self-images that might deter him from the Quest.

Our metaphorical Camelot is a place of fallible people who need occasional forgiveness in order to improve. The knight knows this, because he is one of them.

His humility is based on the fact that he, like everyone else, is only human. He forgives offenses, and hopes to be forgiven in return. This is more than tolerance. It is a social dynamic of mutual pardon and good intent that serves as the foundation of our Camelot dream. We seek to understand human nature, while working steadily to help it evolve. One can liken it to familial love, where differences are overcome by honoring ties of kinship.

The knight-errant no longer has to forgive himself. There is no imaginary *persona* left to forgive. His authenticity leaves no room for that clinging shadow, that bearer of guilt.

He becomes a living expression of his beliefs.

Chapter 15

"Courtesy and Honor..."

Trust # 12: I will live my life with courtesy and honor from this day forward.

The twelfth and final Trust, that of courtesy and honor, comes last for good reason.

Courtesy and honor are not roles that we play, or behavior we adopt in order to win approval. If they were, Chivalry-Now would be a poor philosophy indeed. The qualities we espouse are either authentic, or we are shamed.

This is where the previous Trusts prove their mettle. Each contributes in its own special way to a supportive relationship to one another, almost like building blocks, until courtesy and honor become genuine expressions of our soul. By transforming us into courteous and honorable men, the code draws our truest nature into full expression.

Now that you have explored some of their depth in the preceding chapters, please read the Twelve Trusts again. Reflect not only on their meaning, but on how your own inner light responds to them.

The Twelve Trusts
Upon my honor...

1. I will *develop my life* for the greater good.
2. I will *place character above riches, and concern for others* above personal wealth.
3. I will *never boast,* but cherish *humility* instead.
4. I will *speak the truth* at all times, and forever keep my word.

5. I will *defend* those who cannot defend themselves.
6. I will *honor and respect women*, and refute sexism in all its guises.
7. I will *uphold justice* by being fair to all.
8. I will be *faithful in love* and *loyal* in friendship.
9. I will *abhor scandal and gossip*—neither partake nor delight in them.
10. I will be *generous* to the poor and to those who need help.
11. I will *forgive* when asked, that my own mistakes will be forgiven.
12. I will *live my life with courtesy and honor* from this day forward.

By adhering to the 12 Trusts, I swear to partake in the living **Quest** in everything I do.

It is my hope that this introduction to the Twelve Trusts sparked more than intellectual interest. It should appeal to your heart as well. The Trusts are not negative commandments or regulations. They are *affirmations* of what it means to be a man, affirmations that flow with abundant life when properly received.

The essence of chivalry cannot be found in some book or lost story from a thousand years ago. It exists inside you, or does not exist at all. It cannot be transplanted from one person to another — it can only be awakened.

You know that chivalry has awakened in your heart when courtesy and honor naturally assert themselves in everything you do.

You will start to understand the reason for your discontent. You will discover the purpose, meaning and authenticity that was lacking before. As your completeness comes to life, you will be ready for the adventure that awaits you.

There is nothing overtly mystical about this process. Chivalry-Now is not based on esoteric mumbo-jumbo from a forgotten age. It is a combination of reason and idealism that reaches far back to our cultural past, providing a potent remedy for today's problems.

Our goal is achieved by becoming who we really are, plain and simple. We are complete when we express what is good and sacred in us all — as complete as human beings can be.

Courtesy and honor are not principles of merit that we aspire to. They are the expressions of self-made men who believe in truth, fairness, humility, generosity, forgiveness and sound gender relationships. The Twelfth Trust is not so much a principle, but the culmination of what a true knight-errant is.

***

Courtesy and honor are the life 's blood of the new knight-errant, just as it was for his medieval predecessors. They provide a way for men to socially engage with life while being true to their principles. With honor we are trustworthy, dependable and committed to moral action. With courtesy, we treat people as we should all be treated. Both come from who we are and what we believe. According to medieval chivalry, the man who lacks honor and acts discourteously is disparagingly referred to as a *knave*.

We tend to concentrate on the words *courtesy* and *honor* in this Trust, but there is more. Just as important, perhaps more so in the long run, are the words *I will live…*

The Twelve Trusts are stepping stones to authentic living. They bring our moral and spiritual core to life, which completes who we are in every moment of our experience. In a very real sense, they produce a new life.

***

Courtesy is undervalued and needs to reclaim its previous stature for today's world. For those who wish to help, courtesy starts by being aware of the needs and comfort of others, and responding to them in a genuine fashion. Consideration toward others is of prime importance. Manly self-discipline is the means.

Let us review some of the benefits it brings:

- Courtesy breeds friendship and good will.
- It contributes to social harmony.
- It provides benevolent structure to our relationships.
- It promotes respect and comfort within communities, large and small.
- It proactively dissolves barriers to communication that allows a sharing of different ideas.
- Courtesy encourages self-esteem by honoring the unique value of every person.
- It supports the nobility of human life by recognizing and responding to it at every turn.

This applies to all people, no matter what class, educational level or financial status.

It is appropriate for a man of strength to be civil in discourse and in deed. The benefits are not only social and cultural, they apply directly to the individual as well.

From chivalry's perspective, polite behavior is akin to generosity and provides a strong component for fostering positive gender relationships. It *respects* people's differences rather than *tolerates* them, which borders on insult. It reflects character, and is a true compatriot of valor. It promotes gallantry and trust.

From a personal standpoint, courtesy reflects self-control, confidence and refinement, all noticeable qualities of manly character.

It recognizes gender differences and honors them appropriately, as long as both parties are comfortable with it. It also provides some of the finer aspects to the interplay of love. Nothing is more *natural* or provides greater pleasure than treating a loved one courteously. If that treatment is not forthcoming, something is wrong.

***

Advocating for courteous behavior might seem like a waste of time. Courtesy provides the most ubiquitous human rituals of them all, found in all cultures to varying degrees and expressions. Where people live together, niceties spontaneously occur that eventually become culturally ingrained. Breaches of courtesy are frowned upon, while meeting social expectations is approved. Such common decency is found everywhere, throughout history.

The sad thing is that we do need to advocate for courtesy today. It is noticeably faltering in Western society, despite our wealth of knowledge and supposed sophistication. Our entertainment industry has systematically devalued courtesy over decades. In so doing, it has devalued us as well. Courtesy reflects how we think of one another. Our present day image is not too pleasant.

The danger signs are everywhere. For example, we mostly expect politeness from salespeople who want our money. I have met a number of real estate agents who transform their glum frowns to a smile whenever a customer is near.

"The customer is always right." As benign as that sounds, it shows the first crack in business world authenticity. Courtesy for money. The Japanese Geisha would be proud.

Neighborhoods have become communities of walled-off strangers. Kind words are often used facetiously and spark distrust. "What is he trying to *sell* me? What does he want?" Children make demands of parents, who expect nothing in return — not even respect.

The most obvious contradiction of courteous behavior has to be rap music. The reader might expect the usual diatribe one hears about rap music, how it provokes anti-social attitudes that are harmful to young minds. In truth, there is much to complain about. The language is often foul, overflowing with rage and incivility, along with overt sexuality and criminal undertones. It seems nothing is taboo to rap singers, be it murder, rape, or stealing, accompanied by complete disdain for the system. The ponderous beat, scowling faces and aggressive, vitriolic movements suggest more of a war dance than anything deemed to be entertainment. Anger, accusations and explosive lack of self-control are integral parts of its make-up. The fact that society accepts such displays under the aegis of art, and so many young people buy into it, are sure signs of cultural problems that are being ignored.

As an advocate of Chivalry-Now, however, I find myself unable to condemn rap music — not that I approve of it or like it in any way. What I hear in rap is the clearest expression of cultural male frustration that I can find.

To me, rap singing portrays a powerful indictment of our cultural failures toward the spirit of men. It expresses the futility that most men share, although the majority repress it. Rap singing, whether it realizes it or not, is a rebellion against a society where positive male values have no recognized place of honor. The resulting void is filled with the hypocrisy of empty promises and sham moral dictates that are not applied fairly. Youthful male energy, constantly thwarted, can explode and rebel in terrible ways. We see this illustrated in rap. Bad behavior is glorified, even when it results in death or imprisonment, because it is aimed at a cultural enemy difficult to define or even recognize, but there nonetheless. In a land of plenty, how do we confront a pervasively scourging... *void?*

Rap music's battle cry tells us that we should all be rebelling against this social affront to our gender. There is a cultural war in the West, and it is not between liberals and conservatives as some would have us believe. It is between the cultural needs of half the population versus a soppy, anemic social aimlessness that cares only about market viability. Our value as men cannot be judged by wealth or power. That not only leaves most of us out of the running, it completely ignores the ethical principles that we need to be real men. Ignore them on a grand scale, devalue them, laugh at them all the way to the bank, and a moral rebellion becomes inevitable.

Those who do not rebel, who have had their animus completely trampled into submission, are the ones I pity most. We see them everywhere. Quiet, empty eyes, where hope has long been cancelled. Followers. Their every thought dictated by the expectation of others. Their only goal is retirement. Love is passionless to them, because everything is passionless. They walk around shopping malls straggling behind their wives and girlfriends, looking lost and forgotten. Somewhere along the line, they misplaced their souls and became nameless cogs in a machine.

Despite my dislike for rap music, I recognize how the haunting emptiness of so many of our brothers' lives calls for rebellion, and rap seems to express the resulting anger — for good or for ill. The knight-errant, however, is not so much a rebel as a man dedicated to worthy causes. He knows what rebels forget, that courtesy and honor provide the salve that heals many wounds — whereas complaining, strutting around and breaking the law only makes things worse.

Chapter 16

The Quest

By adhering to the 12 Trusts, I swear to partake in the living Quest in everything I do.

This postscript to the Twelve Trusts refers to a concept that is almost inseparable from chivalry: the *Quest*.

In the musical **Man of La Mancha,** the tavern wench, Aldonza, asks Don Quixote what he means when he refers to *the quest*. In this brief prelude to chivalry's powerful theme song, *The Impossible Dream*, the benevolent madman briefly explains that the quest is:

> "...the mission of each true knight — his duty, nay, his privilege."

Thus he introduces the Impossible Dream as the duty of each knight to apply the code of chivalry in everything he does, while tackling the world's problems on a daily basis. More than just a duty, it is his privilege, it provides him with the kind of purpose and meaning that is natural for a knight. Chivalry inspires the kind of correct living that defines him as such.

The idea of questing is deeply rooted in tales of chivalry. As a literary device, it predictably led Arthurian knights from one harrowing adventure to another.

The medieval quest was analogous to the mythical *hero's journey*, a cultural blueprint for male development. It taught that a boy becomes a man by leaving his family circle and confronting a series of adventures through which he learns vital lessons about himself and the world. The journey ends when he returns home as a man, with the knowledge and experience needed to benefit everyone.

It is a simple theme, but its importance to the male psyche cannot be overstated. It is repeated in almost every myth and legend handed down to us, and is methodically cloned even today in literature and cinematic releases. Popular examples include *Star Wars* and *Lord of the Rings*, which have attracted hungry young males by the millions.

The word *quest* has two primary meanings: that of journeying in search of adventure, and that of a mission, seeking for a person or object. The most famous example of the quest for an object is the quest for the Holy Grail.

Both of these meanings are incorporated into Chivalry-Now as vital elements for today's knight-errant. They represent man's proper attitude and motivation to life itself.

In determining the requirements of manhood, one needs to establish certain criteria as a basic foundation. Chief among these is determining how a man should confront and engage the entire prospect of living in the world. At present, our culture ignores these vitally important lessons. Boys confront the world with big question marks, and then incorporate answers based on what attracts their juvenile interest. Life should be fun, like a game; exciting, like a competition; filled with flickering distractions, like television. They conclude that the world is meant to entertain them and fulfill their wishes. Our broken culture fails to teach otherwise.

There are even some tendencies in religion that enforce that idea. When someone says we should perform good works out of obedience or for the love of God, or to inherit eternal reward, what psychological subtext does that deliver? Talk of obedience, reward and punishment do not elevate virtue so much as generate avarice and fear. Ideas like heaven and hell, Judgment Day, retribution for all eternity, encourage a view of the world based not on virtue, but on what are essentially selfish concerns.

Reward, punishment and fear supply selfish motivations from start to finish. Exploitive commercialism remains poised like a vulture, ready to take full advantage.

Boys and young men deserve far better than this from their culture. Even primitive societies do more, through meaningful traditions and rites-of-passage. They deserve the kind of time-honored, tradition-based directions that society is supposed to furnish to complete them as men.

***

It is the nature of the human mind to know and understand things, and to actively seek knowledge. This is why the search for truth is so vital to Chivalry-Now. It provides the impetus for actualizing who we are and what heights we will attain. When we stop learning, time itself shackles us where we are and leaves us behind.

The Quest (in contrast to a *quest*) of Chivalry-Now provides a comprehensive elaboration for our search for truth. It refers not only to our daily accumulation of knowledge, but to our spiritual growth as well.

The Quest prompts us to find something in particular that has not yet not been defined: an object, person or event that reveals some of the sublime Mystery of Truth. Not knowing what this object, person or event is, or how or when we will find it, we symbolically refer to it as the Grail, that elusive relic of power and plenty that Arthur's knights committed themselves to find. In the end, our mission is not about finding an actual cup or object, but about confronting who we really are in relationship to the world we live in, and making choices between right and wrong.

The Quest prompts us to be aware of the Mystery that eludes our calculating minds, that adds dimensions of the spiritual that cannot be explained, yet underscores everything with meaning. The society we live in is a cold, repetitive, spirit numbing place without it.

The Quest helps to reveal some of the world's Mystery. It tells us how to look for it, assuring us that there is more to life than personal consumption. It challenges us to see things we might not otherwise notice. This engagement with life, physical, emotional, intellectual and spiritual, is the essence of authenticity.

The Quest is an attitude of aliveness, maximizing the experience of life with a constant flow of insight. It is acquiring the abundance of life, even in the midst of poverty. It is conquering fear in order to embrace the grand Mystery we are part of.

The Quest approaches life as it should, as an ongoing adventure from which we learn and grow and hopefully make a positive difference. It honors who we are as human beings and encourages us to be complete. This attitude is fundamental to being a knight-errant. Errantry means freely searching for adventure. It also means working to set things right as part of one's personal journey.

To the medieval mind, this was done for the glory of the knight, or, if he were sufficiently humble, for his king or lady. For us, it is for taking part in the true glory of our species, which is doing what is right for its own sake, without ulterior reasons.

Whether we believe in God or not, the quality of who we are as men depends on the values we believe in — not for juvenile reasons, like reward and punishment, but because we recognize and defend what is right as men.

Anything less is intellectually and spiritually immature.

***

It is hard to describe the full meaning of the Quest, even though most of us intuitively understand it. I will try my best, hoping that readers compensate with their own intuition.

Participating in the Quest provides the kind of immediacy that comes from openness of mind, from seeing things as if for the first time, which carries with it occasional feelings of joy. It is empathizing with the pain of others, which carries feelings of genuine concern. It is the desire to set things right, to protect others and build a better world, which carries passion and indomitable hope. It sparks delight from every success, and new resolve from every failure.

New birth symbolizes the start of new life. What is life, if not the direct experience of your own ever-changing perspective, which in itself connotes a continuum of constant new birth?

This perspective is not achieved by judging solely by the past, but by boldly confronting the present, here and now, fresh and new, with a grasp of personal participation and responsibility.

The knight-errant is a willing servant to his ideals, for such ideals express the man he truly is. Thanks to the Quest, these are not stagnant ideals written in stone that he must follow. They are alive. They grow alongside and within him, driven by the Quest.

It is important to realize that the past is not a window through which we are meant to look for the future. It is a resource to learn from. It is an accumulation of knowledge, a ready reference available to help us build our understanding. This is its purpose, its value. What fails us is when the past, our memories included, obstructs our view of what is, and what the flow of time actualizes at every moment. We need to confront that flow directly, completely unencumbered, in order to experience life at its fullest.

The Quest means opening one's heart and mind to the flow of every moment as it arrives. The adventure comes from seeing the uniqueness of every moment, and responding with integrity. The adventure, the risk if you will, comes from doing what is honorable and right in a world that prefers complacency and scandal.

Here is our calling:

Out of the shadows of the Dark Ages, we come as men of light, men of vision, men of honor, to return what was lost, fix what was broken, and bring life to a pervasive conscience long considered dead. That is our mission. That is our Quest.

***

The Quest can be viewed as chivalry come to life through our daily actions and perceptions.

While the Quest depends on chivalry, chivalry also depends on the Quest. One cannot be separated from the other without detracting from them both. The Quest alone is a journey without direction or goal. Chivalry alone is charade — fine words and noble posturing, but lacking a true manifestation in reality. To be authentic, to be a real knight-errant, you must have both.

The Quest has to do with motivation. Selfless service. Putting yourself in the path of events in order to influence them. Staying aligned with your highest principles, even when trials get rough. Not seeking rewards or even recognition for good deeds. Taking chances. Learning from mistakes. Holding on to one's ideals under adverse conditions.

These qualities reflect more than following a set agenda. They reflect personal ideals that come from the heart that has awakened to itself. This is the conscience and energy of the Quest, and most men feel its pull instinctively.

They may resist. They may reject it as unrealistic. They may laugh at it, but even then something deep inside suffers with regret for missing out on life that is intrinsically real.

In the end, looking back on every success and failure, every initiative and avoidance, when our days and hours are numbered and the sum is tallied, we will know if our lives were worthwhile to the world that spawned us, or just worthwhile to ourselves.

CHAPTER 17

The Knight and His Sword

In certain respect, the knight errant is nothing special. Like every man, he is gifted or impeded by whatever traits form his character.

He cannot be squeezed into any sort of stereotype. The Quest for Truth enhances what is unique in everyone who participates in it and provides its own direction. The process of search and discovery, with its deep experience of every moment, individuates a person. Life becomes a constant source of self-development. Quiet conformity is not the same as humble courtesy.

By recognizing the harmonious diversity of the world he is part of, the knight errant *consciously participates* in its unfolding, its evolution. His search for truth makes him less encumbered by illusion, allowing the personal fulfillment that comes from taking an active and vital role in living.

The most striking attribute of the knight errant is his *basic humanity*. He responds to the pulse of life around him, not dwelling in the past or constantly dreaming of the future. This makes him sensitive to the needs of others, to justice and compassion. Since life is the adventure which defines him at every moment, he is not afraid to respond to challenges that confront him. He is a man of action.

The strength of the knight errant comes from self-development and self-control. He has prepared himself to face life's challenges with honor, integrity, and a will for justice. When wrong, he willingly admits it, and tries to make amends.

Humility enhances his liberation. Courteous to others, he prefers to listen rather than speak, and tries to act appropriately without contradicting his values.

He has respect for women. His capacity for love is not trivialized by romantic themes, but strengthened by the resolve that comes from commitment. The love of a particular woman inspires him to do his best at all times.

His devotion to the quest demands strength of mind and body. This means proper exercise and a healthy lifestyle, avoiding excesses and addictions, associating with good people, rest, good food and clean water. It means taking an interest in things and constantly learning.

The knight errant respects knowledge. He exercises his intellect to expand his understanding of the world. This might be through formal education, book-learning, everyday experience or contemplation — he is a student of life. He knows that intellect is not merely an accumulation of knowledge (which is little more than memory). Intellect is the clarity of perception that is alive to the moment. It includes the power of reason as well as the ability to care. Knowing full well that *ego-pride* is a hindrance to clear thinking, the knight errant prefers the resourcefulness of *human-pride*.

Can someone who is physically or mentally challenged be considered a knight errant?

Of course. As individuals, we are called to reach our fullest potential, whatever that potential might be. The quest, like life itself, challenges everyone. It is our response that makes the difference. Our truest failure is not to try.

Like most of us, the modern knight errant probably works for a living. Doing so, he works to the best of his ability. He never seeks, in any way, to cheat his employer, for he appreciates his daily wage and their mutual commitment. He is punctual and offers constructive advice when appropriate.

He does not cast blame easily. Relationships are difficult to mend when people act negatively to one another. When choosing the proper action, he asks himself: *what is the honorable thing to do?*

This makes him courteous to all. He is not afraid to smile, or converse with strangers.

His commitment to the quest automatically makes him a defender of what is good. This rewards his conscious life with purpose and meaning.

He is supportive of others but cautious not to *impose* his values. Personal example does far more than verbal persuasion.

The knight errant recognizes that freedom encompasses more than just the ability to "do as one pleases." He understands that *freedom* is synonymous with *responsibility*. You cannot have one without the other.

He leads a simple life. He works, has friends, enjoys hobbies. His home is clean and comfortable, but never ostentatious.

He is a good friend, a loving spouse, a concerned father, a dedicated son. To strangers, he is pleasant and courteous, not the least threatening. To his enemies he is relentless yet not abusive, more concerned with truth than with winning. Because of this, even his enemies respect him.

The image that forms is that of a man living up to the obligations of being a man. In this respect, the image beckons to us all, no matter what race chanced to color our skin, no matter what culture formed our background, no matter what our sexual preference. It is how we treat each other that counts.

A collection of such men could change the world. Such was King Arthur's dream. Can you imagine a *Round Table* of bright, intelligent people (not just men), all dedicated to the task of setting things right? I am not talking about representatives of special interests, each with his or her own agenda (that would be far too limited and contentious), but with a single agenda of truth and a desire for action. Think of what this Round Table could accomplish — if only through inspiration.

Instead, we are impeded with a faceless, politically correct, corporate mentality that believes that no one is responsible, no one is to blame — as if the problems of the world just appeared out of nowhere.

Our present system does not encourage true heroes to step forward. There is no door to enter, no castle to storm, no innocent victim to rescue. More often than not, there is no honorable leader deserving of our loyalty and respect. The enemy is faceless. We look for him everywhere, and see only ourselves.

There is reason for that.

The enemy is our own deprivation of heroic self.

***

While reading the tales of King Arthur, years ago, I felt a strong need for a more tactile connection to this medieval warlord. The quiet New England village where I live offers little in the way of communing with the warrior spirit of a thousand years past. Books helped, and I read voraciously. Attending medieval fairs added another dimension. I even turned to the *Society for Creative Anachronism* for this connection, but the meetings were too far away. The more I looked, the more frustrated I became.

It finally occurred to me. If I wanted to know what it felt like to be a knight, I needed a sword. I needed to experience how much it weighed, how it felt in my hand. I wanted to understand its mystical nuance, both in history and legend. We all know that the image of a true knight is inseparable from his sword.

After a fair amount of research, I ordered a sword that promised to be a weapon of true quality.

It arrived by post about a week later. I opened the box with a wonder and excitement I had not felt since childhood. Taking hold of its hilt and lifting it for the first time made me think of young Arthur freeing the sword that made him king.

My new sword was pretty basic. No Excalibur. Even so, I sensed its timeless power, its mystique. Feeling its weight, listening to it slice through the air, was nothing less than thrilling.

Beautiful!

Its flat blade had four narrow grooves, called *fullers,* that extended from the guard to about a third of its length. (Fullers lessen the weight of the sword without depriving it of strength.) The *guard* was also made of steel, slim and pleasingly curved away from my hand. The wooden grip was covered with smooth black leather. Holding the hilt in place was a disk-shaped *pommel,* about two and a half inches in diameter. The pommel's weight provided balance to the entire weapon.

It seemed more beautiful by the moment!

The catalogue I purchased it from actually had a name for it: *Moonshadow.* It was heavier than movies suggest, but not nearly as heavy or as awkward as display swords made from stainless steel. Like the medieval original it was based upon, it was carbon steel, which made the sword tough, flexible and capable of holding a fine edge. I would have to take care to keep it from rusting.

For the next few weeks I remained enthralled by its presence in my home, taking every opportunity to lose myself in a reverie that connected me to the distant past. I sensed some kind of magic in its form — perhaps *empowerment* is a better word. It whispered that it could make all things possible. Defend loved ones. Vanquish enemies. Safeguard what is true and good. Most of all, it could transform my mundane existence into something more exciting and dynamic.

Like the sacred talisman used in a right-of-passage, it offered a gateway to an assemblage of men that traversed the ages. Legendary warriors; heroes and knights; shadows from the Round Table and Valhalla; common soldiers sacrificing their lives for a common cause and a common grave. It was all there, sacrifice and honor, friendship and loyalty. In pure silence it invited me to join their ranks.

At night, under cover of dark, I brought *Moonshadow* outdoors to commune with its enchantment. Standing next to our pond, where moonlight glistened across the dark surface, I would raise the sword like a salute to heaven, sometimes to the moon itself. The silence and liberation of those moments were intoxicating.

I experimented with wielding this incredible weapon, swinging it with long, smooth strokes as if engaging an imaginary opponent. Each motion intensified that connection with warriors past, as if I were tapping into their experiences. I felt some measure of their fear, dedication and perseverance.

After weeks of this "(k)nightly practice," I felt more accustomed to the sword's weight, balance and capabilities. Before I knew it, I was reading books on Western sword fighting, studying illustrations and watching videos on medieval combat. I started to lift weights to build strength.

My indulging wife occasionally practiced with the sword as well. On warm summer nights we did this amid the sounds of bull-frogs and owls. The pond glittered with starlight, like some placid dream of the unconscious. It became my way of honoring the knights of the Round Table, whose ghosts lingered in the shadows around us.

Maybe I was just indulging the child inside me, the long restrained boy who even now wants to fight dragons and unpretentiously embrace high ideals. Despite decades of disenchantment, the innocent dreamer who wants to be a hero still lives.

I am guessing, of course, but I think this inner hero can be found in most men.

***

To describe the subtle magic of a good sword, you need to experience it firsthand. Perhaps what I sensed is a psychological remnant from centuries past, etched in my own genetic psyche. Perhaps it is just imagination gone wild.

I have no desire to harm anyone with this weapon. All I know is that when I practice with it on tranquil nights, awash in lunar glow, I feel more complete and alive, connected to a vast ocean of accumulated male energy otherwise lacking. I feel *kinship* with those ancient warriors, and less vulnerable because of it.

Jesus said that he did not come to bring peace into the world, *but a sword*. What did he mean? He never espoused violence (although much violence was later enacted in his name). What was he trying to say?

I like to think that he once held a sword and sensed the same unity and completeness that I did. Did it represent *action* to him? *Bravery?* A religious *quest?* Did it present some insight into the violence of the world? Perhaps it was the idea of possessing a sword, with all its destructive potential, *and not using it*. Perhaps he wanted the warrior's idea of peace, not through weakness or fear, but through a strong commitment to what is right.

In Arthurian literature, the sword frequently provided mystical and even reverential elements:

- Arthur became king by drawing a sword from a stone. But who or what actually chose him? The sword? The stone? His own strength? Or something else? Legend had it that he was destined to be king. Perhaps Merlin orchestrated the "miraculous" feat to bring this destiny about. Nevertheless, it was Arthur's innocent hand, his own potential for good, his intention to give the sword to someone else, that took hold of the moment and changed his world.
- He later received the magical sword *Excalibur* from the mysterious *Lady of the Lake*. This was a weapon of immense power that assured his success.
- Sir Galahad's sword, reflecting a variation of Arthur's tale, was withdrawn from an anvil that floated on water. His ability to accomplish this feat designated him as the perfect knight.
- There was the beautiful sword of the *Grail King*, cursed to

break when it was needed most.

- Sir Lancelot was inducted as a knight by King Arthur, but did not consider himself a knight until Queen Guenevere sent him a sword and claimed him as her champion.
- Early in Sir Lancelot's career, his mentor, the Lady of the Lake, explained that a sword's double-edge represented the dual responsibilities of defending church and king.
- The symbolism of the *broken sword* that only the saintly Sir Galahad could repair is significant. I believe this symbolized manhood itself, broken in spirit by greed and submission to others. It could only be repaired by someone who best represented the ideals of chivalry.

If we accept that the sword symbolizes manhood, the tales reveal fascinating insights:

- The sword that young Arthur withdrew from the stone stood for the liberation of male ideals previously undeveloped: half stone, half transformed into the symbolic sword, needing the ideal leader to raise it into consciousness.
- Excalibur symbolized the *sovereignty* of male virtues, duly endorsed by female principles (by the Lady of the Lake, who represented the goddess of the Celts). Along with its magical scabbard, it vanquished enemies while protecting whomever wielded it from harm.
- The sword of the Grail King, destined to break when needed most, warns us of the hypocrisy of proclaiming male virtues that we do not adhere to. The hypocrisy of failed ideals can only be repaired by the virtues of our original nature, which Perceval or Galahad symbolized.

The sword remains an appropriate symbol of manhood even to this day, its image sanctified by the blood of a million warriors.

I still sense it. Can you?

***

The metallurgy involved in making a good sword was akin to alchemy and much revered during the Middle Ages. In truth, sword-makers had no real idea why one sword was better than another. The inclusion and amount of carbon as an "impurity" was more the result of accident than anything else. They conjectured that the quality of water during the tempering process might be the answer. (Which might explain why Excalibur was a gift from the Lady of the Lake.)

A decent sword might cost a man a full year's income.

To boys, at least in my time, every fallen branch, yard stick or curtain rod offered the potential for an imaginary sword. It was fun playing with such implements, fun making believe you were wounded, grunting in mock pain, falling to the grass with the certainty of quick and painless resuscitation.

The reality of an actual sword is somewhat different.

It is basically a large knife or cleaver designed to cut or pierce human flesh. It is not for hunting or to cut down trees. Its sole purpose was the butchery of human beings. So much for the fun of childhood play.

Conclusion? *A real sword was and is as serious as life.*

Chivalry (often symbolized by the sword) infuses this same element of meaning into our everyday lives. Life is not a game. Weapons are not toys. Suffering and death are terrible realities we need to deal with.

Chivalry's sword reminds us of that. Accept it, and you embrace a harsh but very lucid vision of the world: seeing things as they really are beyond the façade of illusion.

Life is serious. In many ways it is *tragic.* The consummate party-goer avoids this realization until struck by it unprepared. Tragedy and misfortune have severe ways of dispelling illusions.

The fall of celebrities into alcohol or drug addiction or even suicide bears witness to this truth.

We think of the knight in shining armor, astride his white charger. He seems invincible, fearless, his proud banner fluttering in the wind. That image is little more than an illusion.

His armor was heavy and had a tendency to rust. It limited his motion and would stink after a day or two on the road. Metal plates froze in winter and baked in summer, with him inside. The realities of the medieval world offered few creature comforts. Warriors had to be tough, and the vocation of knighthood added further discomforts and responsibilities. Nevertheless, their warrior spirit often found joy in the midst of struggle. Some wrote songs and poetry. Others played music (such as the fabled Sir Tristan). They indulged in games and tests of skill. Romantic love was not a pastime or diversion, but one of life's imperatives. Their sense of honor stemmed from the very best of human-pride.

In our world, most of the hardships of medieval times have been eradicated. Our homes are blessed with temperature control. Modern medicine has made great strides in eradicating disease and furthering life expectancy. A variety of entertainment is available at the click of a button. Our legal system provides a relatively safe environment. Enemies are not storming the gates. Travel is comparatively safe, fast, and comfortable.

Why then, in such a world of comfort and convenience, does joy so readily escape us? How is it that so many of us turn to drugs and alcohol just to cope with our daily lives, knowing full well we are only making things worse?

Perhaps we are not challenged to take life seriously enough to boldly engage in it. Perhaps meaningless distractions push aside what really has meaning. Perhaps, as a culture, we have forgotten the quest that once defined us.

More and more we live in a commercialized world that

devalues the very qualities that make us humane. Being disconnected from time-honored definitions of manhood, we suffer from an emptiness which our wonderful technology can neither compensate for nor fully anesthetize us from.

There is a quote from the John Boorman's movie, *Excalibur,* that amply illustrates this point. King Arthur, portrayed as the Wounded King, is given to drink from the *Holy Grail.* One sip immediately heals him, both body and soul. He turns to Sir Perceval with new energy in his eyes:

"I didn't know how empty was my soul, until it was filled."

This statement summarizes our existential situation as men. We are so removed from our basic nature that we can scarcely recognize what is missing. All we do know is the constant discontent that propels us to our next train of distractions.

We turn to psychoanalysis to alleviate an ache that has no simple cure. Little things in our past haunt us with a barrage of neuroses. Why? Because they were never resolved, the analyst will say. That's true. But even more importantly, in terms of Chivalry-Now, neither were they replaced by a maturing life filled with purpose and meaning.

A stark, almost morbid question faces us: is it even possible to restore and maintain the essence of manhood in the world we live in today?

One might argue that the essence of manhood is alive and well, straining muscles at the nearest weight-room, bouncing a ball across the gym floor, dancing suggestively in local nightclubs. We see them in beer commercials, virile and masculine, and for the most part uncaring. Our world is filled with so-called *masculine* images: the Marlborough man. Actors on television. Stone-faced policemen. Professional wrestlers.

Is that it? Are these two-dimensional images really what manhood is all about?

Look around. There are those who think they are men who refuse to support their own children, or act like fathers in bringing them up. There are men who cheat on their wives without an ounce of remorse. Many are addicted to the numb security of alcohol or drugs, or rot away in prison because they were not man enough to live honest and productive lives. Too many women are battered, harassed, and discriminated against by so-called men. Too many politicians play mind games with the public for their own gain. There is too much meaningless war and violence. Too much welfare, tax evasion, and insurance fraud. Too many lawsuits, bankruptcy appeals, accidents on the highway, high school dropouts, teenage pregnancies. We have to face the sorry truth: most thieves, murderers and other criminals are men.

Now, ask yourself why?

If the essence of manhood were alive and well, the results would be different. There would be positive teamwork among politicians; more families that are stable and independent; more boys and girls with fathers they can rely on; more women who feel secure not only on the streets or in job interviews, but in their own homes.

Best of all, a man's character would be more valued than his image.

How do we reclaim what it means to be a man?

We start by opening our eyes and seeing what real manhood requires:

- It is manly to be honest at all times, a searcher and respecter of truth.
- It is manly to help those in genuine need.
- It is manly to fight for what is right.
- It is manly to be courteous to everyone.
- It is manly to honor women, and by doing so honoring life itself.

- It is manly to work hard, always doing the best you can.
- It is manly to be responsible to one's family, community, nation and world.

LIKEWISE:

- It is *not* manly to lie.
- It is *not* manly to belittle or bully another person.
- It is *not* manly to complain all the time. When necessary, make your protest heard, or share your grief with a friend who cares. To constantly complain is to let what troubles you dominate your life.
- It is *not* manly to shout down your opponent. That is a sign of weakness. If your concern is truth, make sure that your opponent is well heard. Open your mind to other opinions.
- For the same reason, it is *not* manly to interrupt or dominate a conversation.
- It is *not* manly to be a braggart, lecher, or user of people.
- Last, but not least, smoking cigarettes and drinking alcohol have **nothing** to do with being a man, despite all the Hollywood glamorizing and commercial reinforcement. There are few things that effectively ruin a man more than these addictive substances, which proves how easily we succumb to lies.

CHAPTER 18

Dualism

Chivalry-Now derives much of its power by appealing to the *original nature* of men, what might also be called their moral center or conscience. We are born with the potential for this inner discernment, but we all develop and respond to it differently.

Some pay it heed and build honorable lives that ring with authenticity; some ignore it in favor of all the distractions that compete for our attention; others try to suppress it in order to assert control over their lives — even though they suppress the better part of who they are.

Call it instinct, intuition or just a natural part of growth, this original nature calls us with the longing to become real men. Our culture is supposed to contribute to and facilitate this process, but it no longer does. Instead, it purposely hampers our natural inclinations through competing values and constant distraction.

How can we know that this connection between Chivalry-Now and what we call our moral center is real? I can only attribute it to personal experiences that we all have. Not only have I experienced it in my own life, but I have seen it in men's eyes, a spark that fans into living flame at the mention of chivalry. Something awakens, like a yearning akin to nostalgia, a hidden persona stirred to consciousness that has access to a primal vision. A moment's discourse usually prompts comparison with today's amoral society. It concludes with agreement that our culture no longer serves the systematic growth of real men.

The foundation of this philosophy is the assertion that man's nature is basically good. This assumes a fundamental and far reaching difference from those who assert the opposite.

During the Age of Enlightenment, free thinking philosophers

were inspired by human potential, especially our capacity for reason. Their belief in human goodness lent itself to a progressive view of the world, which resulted in the development of democracy and human rights that we know today. It inspired such well-known phrases as *the pursuit of happiness*, and *unalienable rights*. Wherever this energy inspired educated people, a movement transpired that encouraged science, tolerance and the value of every human being.

Age of Enlightenment ideals had to contend with a very different view of humanity. That of *dualism*. This claimed that only spiritual things are good, which necessitated that physical things, like human beings, are bad. Various sects of Christianity arose that propagated this belief in what has been called the Second Great Awakening. The Age of Enlightenment, also known as the Age of Reason, soon came to its demise, although some of its legacy, minus the enthusiasm, survives.

Dualism's disregard for "the flesh" claimed that humanity was sinful to the core, with no viable moral center or inclination toward what is good. Human nature therefore had to be controlled, even rejected as far as possible, in order to maintain a strict social order. The blueprint for control was taken from selected quotes from the bible, and relied heavily on reward and punishment.

The fundamental differences between these two modes of thinking were enormous.

The first looked upon the world with an enthusiasm for learning, a desire to make things better, a fundamental optimism toward human nature that sings with promise.

The second viewed everything in the world as evil and committed itself to stemming the flow of change, afraid that the instigation of any manmade change to the status quo would bring dangerous results.

Whereas the first encouraged people to value freedom and think for themselves, the second was determined to regulate everything by its own tradition, and view diverse thinking as demonically inspired. It looked to scripture for answers to everything and completely abhorred science as a threat, resisting such benign advancements as inoculations against smallpox.

The search for truth that we refer to as the *quest*, which instigates a growing appreciation of both the world and Mystery, is severely hampered when limited to fixed tradition and the teachings of a single book. Nature is ignored. The dynamic of justice is transformed into legalism. The humility it espouses is not an open vision of the world, where ego is set aside to allow direct experience. It is just the opposite, something locked, closed, degrading, and resentful.

One is not called to develop himself for the greater good, but concerns himself with whatever is necessary to acquire salvation in the afterlife. Truth is thought to completely transcend reason, and so reason itself is devalued as something misleading and dangerous. The *Scopes Monkey Trial* illustrates this belief.

Deny the beneficence of conscience, and every variant thought or judgment is held suspect. Rules are never questioned, only obeyed.

Dualism purports that people are made of two distinctly different substances: the physical body and the incorporeal spirit. The spirit, or soul, is considered corrupted by the flesh. Because we are evil, we cannot improve this condition or find salvation on our own, so why try? Only faith can save us, or as the strict Calvinist would have it, God's indeterminable preference as found in predestination.

Such incredible defeatism, which is not accepted by many forms of Christianity, is the antithesis of Chivalry-Now. To refute its negative premise, I present a simple consideration.

Anyone who has brought a child into the world, and witnessed that child's first smile, knows in his or her heart that humanity is good. The love one instantly feels is real, and not imposed from the outside. It comes from within, from the person's own natural instinct. There is no evil in one's heart at such moments. Only love, wonder, appreciation and good will.

Other examples are abundant from everyday life. It is this font of inner goodness that Chivalry-Now recognizes and points to an expression of original nature, or what we simply refer to as conscience.

That being said, I cannot deny that there is moral duality in the world. That would be foolish, considering all we see around us. But this is very different from dualism. The duality we see is not a fixed condition derived from flesh that cannot be altered. It is a consequence of our own making, caused by not following our better instincts — an apparently self-fulfilling prophecy of dualism, augmented by a lack of positive ideals. We have the capacity to reject it for something better.

Human nature is not perfect, but imperfection is a far cry from being evil. Yes, we are weak. Yes, we make mistakes. Yes, we are easily led astray. But our inner light is worthy of being nurtured. We can be better than our apathy suggests. Stronger. More honest. More supportive of the world we are part of. We can define ourselves by more than greed and the lust for power.

The trouble is, we live in a state of competing and contradictory values that feed into the premise of dualism. The cultural despondency that results impedes our ability to respond as conscience would dictate. Some of our best efforts are compromised by conflicting motives that lead to moral and intellectual stagnation.

***

There is evil in the world — and it is usually of our own making. It is our duty not to accept, but to contend with it. Unfortunately, dualism is so firmly and negatively entrenched in this society that it hampers all our efforts.

We live in a world that has embraced a symbiotic cooperation between good and bad in the name of freedom and profit. Our moral sense has been anesthetized to it. The glossed over *bad* has become a protected part of the equation because we can no longer see it as separate. Indeed, in certain respects we become dependent on it, and even defend it as if it were vital to our freedom.

As individuals, how can we contend with this?

With the only weapon that we have. *Truth.*

The flame of truth that each of us carries may be small in comparison to the entrenched illusions of power. Some might consider it insignificant. But the advantage of this flame is that it is real in comparison to the illusions that dominate us. Truth is what it is, and does not waver. It speaks to the heart as nothing else can, and the heart often responsd instinctively. Such purity cannot be bought, turned around or completely snuffed out. Only ignored — as so many of us do now. It resurrects itself with each child's birth, each adolescent's moment of wonder, each adult's sudden moral revelation, and expresses itself with the longing to build a real Camelot.

The knight-errant of Chivalry-Now enjoys single-minded resolve as he faces the challenges of his quest. When he sees the greater good and recognizes his kinship to it, the shackles of duality crumble in his hand. He understands that moral decisions can be complex sometimes, with many shades of grey. He accepts that as part of life. In this way, his vision is clearer than most, allowing him to rise above the conflict of duality. He stays on course, his principles cutting through illusions like a sharpened sword. He is a complete man.

In this way, Chivalry-Now nurtures the seed of Camelot that exists in every man's heart. It is our responsibility to protect that seed and believe in it, so that it grows into a tall, strong tree of life, with branches reaching out in all directions.

CHAPTER 19

The Future of Chivalry-Now

I was asked to give a speech introducing Chivalry-Now back in early 2007. My wife, was kind enough to preface the speech with the following words:

Imagine!

Imagine, for a moment, the sweet dream of civility, strength and compassion that a new form of chivalry could spawn in our enlightened age. A place where men and women respect each other not just for their similarities, but for their symbiotic differences as well. A world where equality is more than just a campaign slogan.

Imagine!

Imagine men whose strengths are dedicated to the betterment of all rather than their own advancement. Imagine politicians who reject spin and disinformation and partial truths, and respect us enough to speak from the heart.

Grace and human dignity would result in cleaner, safer cities. Responsibility and love for life would protect the air we breathe and water we drink. Reason would replace violence. Patriotism would guide us to raise the poor from hunger, and safeguard the health of all people.

Justice would bring fairness to all our dealings, and conquer the lure to cheat. Loyalty would make friendships more true. Romantic love would not be fleeting or shallow. Men could be proud to be men, and women proud to be women.

Imagine!

Imagine a world where personal virtue is so common that no one could deny our way of life its place as an example of true morality.

Imagine men who are more concerned about making their nation proud of them, than boasting about their own patriotic pride.

We can only transform society by transforming ourselves — one person at a time. Not through coercion. Not through propaganda. But through inspiration.

By appealing to what is best in us all.

***

The future is impossible to know.

Thoughts, words and ideas sometime move mountains, while at other times they pass like a quiet breeze. Who can say what will be etched permanently in the lives of many? Or will change the lives of the significant few? Gold is thought precious because we think it so, while time, that which truly is precious, slips through our fingers, and we scarcely notice our lives pass with it.

Chivalry-Now points to solutions that can heal the world we live in. These solutions are not costly. They are not extreme. They lead, potentially, to each man's fulfillment, to peace and sanity, and steering our own evolution back on course.

Chivalry-Now can only fail if *we fail* through our own complacency. When we pronounce that petty greed is more important than the greater good, that frivolous pleasure is enough to stop us from being the men we should be, we blaspheme the universe we are part of. The warrior spirit of the past no longer exists, for we have removed ourselves from that legacy.

Yet even now, in the earliest stages of outreach and advocacy, Chivalry-Now articulates its message. More precisely, men are responding to the ethical longings of their souls when they hear the words and recognize that ageless call. Men all around the world, bright, articulate men of conscience, are responding from the depths of their souls for the greater good that so many of us ignore. Women have also recognized and encouraged this phenomenon, sensing how their own fate is intrinsically entwined.

Chivalry-Now has struck a nerve in the conscience of a growing number of men who realize that something vital, long missing, has suddenly been recovered, and envelops who they are. Its language is instinctively understood. Chivalry-Now belongs to these men. The fate of all men, and the human race in general, is in their hands, and maybe yours as well.

Gentlemen and ladies, the Round Table of sanity awaits us to take our places through commitment, dialog, and perpetuating good deeds. It bids us to make a choice: will humanity rise to the glory it is capable of? Or scourge the earth like a pestilence until the earth itself finds ways of stamping us out? Are we building a shining City on a Hill? Or a seething Wasteland where the Grail no longer resides?

Ladies and gentlemen, we are destroying ourselves along with every virtue we desecrate, and every problem we ignore. We do this with eyes wide open, and minds titillated by greed.

Ask yourself why?

Why not stop, and fix things while we can?

***

Chivalry-Now has become a battle cry for the awakening conscience of men. From this energy a new knighthood emerges, a corps of free men and women who are resurrecting what it means to be authentic.

We have seen epochs in the past where the inspiration of human potential rose and spread like wildfire, transforming the world as it did so. Classical Greece, the Renaissance, the Age of Enlightenment. These were epochs that provided evolutionary leaps in our culture that shaped the entire future. Each of them combined science, art, reason and idealism in uniquely energized fashions. Without them, we would have no science as we know it today, no freedom, no democracy, no critical thinking. We would lack the progressive nobility of the Western spirit. A type of chivalry contributed to each of these epochs, from Stoicism in ancient Greece, to the intellectual challenges that fashioned the Enlightenment. The energy of realistic idealism made all these things possible.

Can we instigate that again? Can Chivalry-Now, or something like it, usher in a new Renaissance, a new Age of Reason and Compassion? Will it help us to escape from the path of destruction we have long been treading?

The future is impossible to know.

We look at the present and guess at possibilities, but only actions make the difference that we need.

The essence of Chivalry-Now depends on you and me and the warrior spirit in us all. Shall we sit on our hands while corporate dragons transform billions of people into servants of greed? Shall we fearfully complain about global warming even as we fuel its continuation? Shall we expand the world's population until the numbers and associated problems become insurmountable? Dare we cling to the obvious error that continued economic growth will eventually solve all our problems, while it strongly contributes to them instead?

Chivalry-Now allows us to care, because it asserts the value of people over money and power, while lifting people up at the same time.

Chivalry-Now is not a dream or hope or intellectual idea that touches on nostalgia. It is not just this book you are reading, or the web site that accompanies it. It is man's spirit reawakened and active again. It is each of us who responds to what is in our hearts as men.

Epilogue

If you have read this book with an open heart and mind, the words should have spoken to you as no other words could — they are words your soul has longed to hear since early childhood, but was denied.

You may have read them at arm's length, treating them as mere text, and remained untouched. You may resist their message as proposing something too radical from the way you live. The words might instigate discomfort, juxtaposed against the lifestyle you embrace. All these responses are possible and ultimately your choice. I thank you for reading this book anyway.

There is a possibility, however, that while you read these words your heart responds with the excitement of returning home from a lengthy exile, finding your inheritance waiting, and loved ones welcoming you with open arms.

Here you find your true name and title, your ancestors and traditions held in high honor, the stronghold that has waited for you for a thousand years. Some family member, an uncle perhaps, explains the nobility you always sensed, but never understood. While in exile, you were a slave or servant, controlled by others, belittled, made to look ridiculous.

And now, suddenly, you are reborn. Or are you?

The long exile you came from summons you back with the promise of familiarity. It is no small step from slavery to knighthood, even when your heart cries out for nothing less. Propaganda from the past has to be let go.

This analogy describes how you are living a familiar archetype of myth. From this point on, you face the future just as mythical heroes always do, having to decide which direction to take. Turn this way, and you continue your priceless journey. Turn that, and you blend into the scenery, a nondescript token of a man who had his chance but turned away.

What you do with Chivalry-Now is up to you. Shutting it away in your heart helps no one, liberates no one — especially you. Trying to balance it with contradictory values only adds to the conflict of duality. The two cannot mix.

You have a decision to make.

I suggest you go to a quiet place and contemplate the meaning of your life. Are you so happy, so sure of the direction you have been on, that staying the course seems the only reasonable path? Or is that still, small voice of conscience no longer still and quiet as before? Has Chivalry-Now provoked it sufficiently to demand its rightful place?

This is what new birth requires. Liberation demands that you re-examine everything you cling to from the past in order to enjoy the clarity of new vision.

If you find yourself so moved… if you long for authenticity… I invite you to embark on your own personal Quest.

Have you embarked already? Then please, stay the course on which the particulars of your life have laid before you. The adventure is already yours. The risk as well. Every adventure has risks. The authenticity of life is measured by them.

If it is any solace, know that you are not alone.

There is a growing community of men and women who are utilizing Chivalry-Now as it relates to their own journeys of truth and honor. Each person who joins them brings us one step closer to realizing our dream of Camelot, a world where honor and sanity reign supreme.

We invite you to our ranks, to our international Round Table of free and independent thinkers, that has no circumference.

For more information, see
www.chivalrynow.net

BOOKS

O is a symbol of the world, of oneness and unity. In different cultures it also means the "eye," symbolizing knowledge and insight. We aim to publish books that are accessible, constructive and that challenge accepted opinion, both that of academia and the "moral majority."

Our books are available in all good English language bookstores worldwide. If you don't see the book on the shelves ask the bookstore to order it for you, quoting the ISBN number and title. Alternatively you can order online (all major online retail sites carry our titles) or contact the distributor in the relevant country, listed on the copyright page.

See our website www.o-books.net for a full list of over 500 titles, growing by 100 a year.

And tune in to myspiritradio.com for our book review radio show, hosted by June-Elleni Laine, where you can listen to the authors discussing their books.

mySpiritRadio